Cranbury
Public
Library

23 North Main St. • Cranbury, NJ 08512
(609) 655-0555

JEFF
BEZOS

Business Executive and Founder of Amazon.com

Bernard Ryan, Jr.

Ferguson
An imprint of ☑® Facts On File

Jeff Bezos: Business Executive and Founder of Amazon.com

Ferguson
An imprint of Facts On File, Inc.
132 West 31st Street
New York NY 10001

Library of Congress Cataloging-in-Publication Data

Ryan, Bernard, 1923-
  Jeff Bezos : business executive and founder of Amazon.com / Bernard Ryan, Jr.
    p. cm.
  Includes bibliographical references and index.
  ISBN 0-8160-5890-3 (alk. paper)
  1. Bezos, Jeffrey—Juvenile literature. 2. Amazon.com (Firm)—History—Juvenile literature. 3. Booksellers and bookselling—United States—Biography—Juvenile literature. 4. Businessmen—United States—Biography—Juvenile literature. 5. Internet bookstores—United States—History—Juvenile literature. 6. Electronic commerce—United States—History—Juvenile literature. I. Title.
  Z473.B47R93 2005
  381'.45002'02854678—dc22

                                                                    2004012155

Ferguson books are available at special discounts when purchased in bulk quantities for businesses, associations, institutions, or sales promotions. Please call our Special Sales Department in New York at (212) 967-8800 or (800) 322-8755.

You can find Ferguson on the World Wide Web at http://www.fergpubco.com

Text design by David Strelecky

Pages 105–121 adapted from Ferguson's *Encyclopedia of Careers and Vocational Guidance, Twelfth Edition*

Printed in the United States of America

MP TB 10 9 8 7 6 5 4 3 2 1

This book is printed on acid-free paper.

CONTENTS

1

AN INCREDIBLY CHARMING MAN

It was late evening, a few days before Christmas in 1997. At the busy Flash Foods convenience store on Amelia Island, a vacation resort in Florida, the counter clerks saw three men dash in. They looked like everyday tourists. But they carried walkie-talkies. One stopped at the door as if guarding it. He seemed to be whispering code words into his radio. Another darted to a position in the check-out line as he radioed code words like "Tango" and "Bravo" to the others. The third ran to the dairy case, grabbed a quart of milk, and raced it to the man in line. That one seemed to have a strange code name: Ffej Sozeb. He paid for the milk. In an instant, the three were out the door, into a white SUV driven by a woman, and were off down the road.

Ffej Sozeb was Jeff Bezos (his name spelled backwards). The guard at the door was his father, Mike Bezos. The raider who bought the milk was Jeff's brother, Mark. The driver was their mother, Jackie Bezos. They were playing one of their favorite games: pretending to be Navy SEALs on a do-or-die raid.

Witnesses of the game could have told you that Ffej Sozeb was a brown-eyed, somewhat balding 33-year-old

Jeff Bezos, founder and chief executive of Amazon.com, became one of the world's wealthiest people by age 33.
(Associated Press)

in khaki slacks and a powder-blue button-down shirt. They would have remembered him by his loud, exuberant laugh, for he did seem to be having such a good time. But no one in that store was aware that the spirited milk-buyer was in fact the man who thought up the highly successful Internet venture Amazon.com and made it work. Nor did they know that in only a couple of years, Amazon.com had made Bezos one of the world's wealthiest people. His worth at that time was some $178 million.

A New Mexico Native

Jeffrey Preston Bezos was born on January 12, 1964, in Albuquerque, New Mexico. His name (pronounced BAY-zohs) comes from the Spanish word *besos*, meaning *kisses*. His mother, Jackie Gise, was married at 17 but divorced soon after Jeff's birth. His grandfather, Lawrence Preston Gise (who was always called Preston), was appointed by the U.S. Congress as manager of the western region of the Atomic Energy Commission (AEC). He was responsible for laboratories in Sandia, Lawrence Livermore, and Los Alamos, where 26,000 people worked.

Jeff's mother met Mike Bezos while she worked in an Albuquerque bank. He was a native of Cuba who had been one of more than 14,000 children brought to the United States between 1960 and 1962 in Operation Pedro Pan

(Peter Pan)—a rescue mission in Miami, Florida, that placed children in foster care. Living in Delaware, Mike Bezos learned English, earned his high school diploma, moved on to college at the University of Albuquerque, and got a job at the bank where he later met Jackie.

Determined, Even at Three

By the time Jeff was three, his mother knew she had an extremely smart and determined son on her hands. He was asking for a real bed rather than the crib he still slept in. She said no. Soon she found him using a screwdriver to take his crib apart. And it was not long before the teachers in Jeff's Montessori school told her they had never seen such concentration in a child. They often found it impossible to distract Jeff from his current task, so to get the boy to move from one activity to another they simply picked up his chair with him in it and moved it to the next assignment.

Mike Bezos and Jackie Gise married in 1968 and Mike adopted Jeff. Jeff's half-sister, Christina, was born in 1970, and his half-brother, Mark, in 1971. The family lived first in Houston, Texas, where Mike worked as a petroleum engineer for Exxon.

Jeff was 10 when Mike and Jackie told him that Mike was not his natural father. The news did not bother him at all. "It's a fine truth to have out there," he said later on.

"I'm not embarrassed by it. As far as I'm concerned, my Dad is my natural father. The only time I ever think about it, genuinely, is when a doctor asks me to fill out a form."

An Early Interest in Technology

By the time he was 10, Jeff was spending summers in southwest Texas on the ranch of his beloved grandfather, Preston Gise. Known to Jeff as "Pop," he had retired near the small town of Cotulla, west of San Antonio and near the Mexican border. His keen technical mind and his devotion to his grandson made Pop Gise an ideal mentor for a boy whose own mind welcomed every gadget he could get his hands on.

Pop Gise recognized in his grandson a fellow scientist, young as he was, and never failed to bring along educational toys and games when he came to visit. He helped his grandson build Heathkit amateur radios and contributed to a growing collection of paraphernalia that threatened to burst the walls of the Bezos garage. Among the projects in various stages of construction or development were an old Hoover vacuum cleaner on the way to becoming a simple hovercraft and an open umbrella that, dressed in aluminum foil, was part of an experiment in solar cooking. "His projects became more complex with age," said Jeff's mother, "but unfortunately the garage never got any bigger."

She did draw the line, however. Jeff, not yet in high school, announced that he had to have a contraption called an Infinity Cube, in which motorized mirrors gave the viewer the sense of staring into infinity. Finding that it cost $20, Mrs. Bezos said no, it was too expensive. For well under $20, Jeff rounded up all the needed parts and built the cube for himself. Jeff also made a bedroom burglar alarm that would alert him if either of his siblings went there.

But not everything in his young life was technical. Like many kids, he naturally wanted to play football even though he had a slight build. His parents enlisted him in the youth league—for boys not yet in high school—where his weight was just enough to get him in. They worried that the bigger boys would squash him, but soon learned that the coach had made Jeff the captain of the defensive team. When they asked why, the coach explained that Jeff carefully memorized not only his assignment on every play but everybody else's, too.

Before Jeff entered high school, Exxon transferred Mike Bezos and his family to Miami, Florida. Now a young teenager, Jeff got plenty of physical exercise during his summers on the Cotulla ranch. There Pop Gise taught him how to use an arc welder and lay irrigation pipe, fix windmills and pumps, build a barn, work cattle on horseback and take them to auction, and rope calves and brand them with his grandfather's LAZY G (the ranch's symbol). One summer the ranch's big D6 Caterpillar bulldozer broke down. Studying a pile of mail-order manuals three feet high, Jeff helped Pop fix it. "On a ranch in the middle of nowhere," he later said, "you have to have a lot of patience."

Jeff's mother echoed his attitude. Thinking about how her son's experience on the ranch taught him to make his own decisions and rely on himself, she later said that one of the things he learned "is that there really aren't any problems without solutions. Obstacles are only obstacles if you think they're obstacles. Otherwise, they're opportunities."

"Very focused on people"

One opportunity Jeff seized while in high school was a competition sponsored by the National Aeronautics and Space Administration (NASA). The prize was a trip to visit NASA's Marshall Space Flight Center in Huntsville, Alabama. Jeff won the trip by writing a paper on "The Effect of Zero Gravity on the Aging Rate of the Common Housefly."

In his junior year in Miami's Palmetto High School, Jeff met a senior named Ursula Werner. "I was taken with him probably from the moment I met him," she later said. "He's an incredibly charming man. He is very focused on people when he's with them. He has one of the most wonderful senses of humor of almost anyone I've met. But unlike some people who have a terrific sense of humor, he can appreciate someone else's sense of humor. I love the way he laughs. It's something I will always remember about him."

Jeff and Ursula dated often, and on her 18th birthday (on March 11, 1981) he told her he had spent days getting her birthday present ready. It was a scavenger hunt, with clues all over the city of Miami. Years later, Ursula remembered that birthday:

> As an indication of how much trouble he went to, he hid one clue under a railroad tie on an old part of the railroad track on South Dixie Highway. He hid another clue under a toilet bowl lid on the sales floor of Home Depot. He had gone to a teller at one of the banks and told her, "When someone comes in on March 11, she will ask you for a million dollars in one dollar bills; give her this clue." It was amazing. Aside from the birth of my three children, I can't ever remember when I've had such an exhausting experience. The world around Jeff Bezos is filled with terrific stories like that because he has such a creative and playful mind.

Jeff, seen here shaking hands with an Amazon.com shareholder, is famous for his warm personality as well as his business smarts. (Landov)

Cracking Eggs with One Hand

During the summer of 1981, when he was 17, Jeff worked as a fry-cook in a Miami McDonald's. There he first learned the importance of customer service, though he himself did not serve the customers. "They wouldn't let me anywhere near the customers," he said years later. "This was my acned-teenager stage. They were like, 'Hmm, why don't you work in the back?' One of the great gifts I got from that job is that I can crack eggs with one hand. My favorite shift was Saturday morning. The first thing I would do is get a big bowl and crack 300 eggs into it. One of the things that's really fun about working at McDonald's is to get really fast at all of this stuff. See how many eggs you can crack in a period of time and still not get any shell in them."

By his senior year in high school, Jeff Bezos had been elected president of his class and had already won Palmetto High's Best Science Student award in his sophomore and junior years and the Best Math Student award in his junior year. He won them again in his senior year, taking also another top honor, the science prize in the Silver Knight competition among all high school students in south Florida. Sponsored by the *Miami Herald* newspaper, the competition involved tough interviews by a panel of experts plus written essays and overall academic achievement. At graduation time, Jeff had the highest marks among 680 students and was named valedictorian of his class.

The *Miami Herald* reported Jeff's thought-provoking valedictory speech. In the speech, Jeff proposed to make the future safe for the human race by making the colonization of space our country's first priority. He advised that we should not consider our future as limited to our planet, for it could be struck at any time by some foreign object from outer space. He also said his hope was to see the construction of a vast commercial space station that included hotels, space yachts, amusement parks, and homes for two or three million people as they orbited the earth. The valedictorian's idea, reported the newspaper, "is to get all people off the Earth and see it turned into a huge national park."

Miami Herald editors kept an eye on the Palmetto valedictorian. That summer of 1982, their reporters described Jeff Bezos's first business venture. He and his girlfriend, Ursula Werner, launched a summer-education camp they named the DREAM Institute (for "Directed REAsoning Methods"). Charging $150 for a two-week program that ran from Jeff's room at home, they signed up five students from fourth, fifth, and sixth grades. "We don't just teach them something," Jeff told the *Herald* reporter, "we ask them to apply it." The curriculum ranged from how a camera works to talks on the limitation of nuclear arms, and from fossil fuels to black holes and electric currents. Reading material included *Watership Down, The Lord of the Rings, Gulliver's Travels, The Once and Future King, Our Town, Stranger in a Strange Land,* and *Treasure Island.*

Jeff and Ursula put his computer and printer to work to create a pamphlet that they distributed to DREAM Institute parents. It promised that their program "emphasizes the use of new ways of thinking in old areas." Little did Jeff know, as he packed up and departed for his freshman year at Princeton University, how well that line described his own future.

2

FROM HONORS STUDENT TO VICE PRESIDENT

As he headed for Princeton, Jeff Bezos was expecting to study electrical engineering and business administration. At the same time, however, his longtime fascination with space exploration kept nagging at him. Two of history's most brilliant physicists—Albert Einstein and Stephen Hawking, both of whom had changed worldwide thinking about the cosmos—were among his favorite scientists. He decided to become, like them, a theoretical physicist. (Theoretical physics is the study of what could be or might be in the physical world, either in the tiniest micro-scopic elements or in the vastness of space.)

Jeff's faculty adviser and the chairman of Princeton's department of physics looked at Jeff's high school records. They reviewed his application for admission to the university. They considered the superb work he had done in his fresh-man classes. Finally, they welcomed him into the honors physics program, where he was one of the top 25 students.

Brains Wired Differently

Jeff went to work in advanced physics courses. Soon he realized that he was laboring among genuine geniuses. He later described the experience: "I looked around the room, and it was clear to me that there were three people in the class who were much, much better at it than I was, and it was much, much easier for them. It was really sort of a startling insight, that there were these people whose brains were wired differently."

Jeff then decided to switch his major. A degree in com-puter science and electrical engineering, he realized, would be just fine. For his senior thesis—an approximately 100-page paper required of every Princeton student before he or she can earn a degree—he designed and built a spe-cial-purpose computer that could do complex calculations needed in analyzing DNA.

Summer Jobs Helping Exxon and IBM

While Jeff was in college, Exxon transferred his father, Mike Bezos, to Norway. Jeff spent the summer of 1984 in that country's town of Stavanger, working as a programmer/analyst for Exxon. Using an IBM computer, he set up a financial plan that made it easy to determine oil royalties—that is, the shares of the profits that are paid to the owners of land containing oil by the company that drills for it.

The next summer, 1985, Jeff worked for IBM in its Santa Teresa Research Labs in San Jose, California. That job gave him the pleasure of adding the following techno-speak to his resume: "In three days, completed a project allocated four weeks for completion, re-implementing IBM software productivity tool user interface by writing exec routine to automatically and selectively change the productivity tool." In other words, he did a four-week job in only three days, and in the process he fixed an IBM system so it worked better.

By the time he graduated summa cum laude from Princeton in 1986, Jeff had been elected to the national honor society Phi Beta Kappa. His grade point average (GPA) in his department was 4.2 (at Princeton, an A+ is 4.3) and his overall GPA for his total academic record was 3.9.

During his senior year, Jeff met recruiters from a number of well-known companies who came to the campus to interview possible future employees. Before he graduated, he turned down offers from at least three that liked his student record: Andersen Consulting (a division of Arthur Andersen, one of the nation's top accounting firms), Bell Laboratories (a descendent of the old Bell Telephone Company), and Intel (the leading maker of microprocessor chips, the brains of personal computers [PCs]).

Not satisfied with offers from such big, established firms, Jeff kept looking around. Then one day he saw a full-page advertisement in the student newspaper, the *Daily Princetonian*. The advertiser was a new company called FITEL that was creating a computer network to handle international financial business. Based in Manhattan, FITEL wanted to talk with Princeton's best computer science graduates.

Commuting between New York and London

Immediately after graduating from Princeton in May 1986, Jeff Bezos became employee number 11 at FITEL. His title was manager of administration and development. This meant that he was in charge of the company's telecommunications network, which stretched worldwide. It used computer programs to connect a complex web of people and companies—such as stockbrokers, investors, and banks—whose business involved transferring data from one country to another on the buying and selling of stocks and bonds.

Only eight months later, in February 1987, FITEL management promoted Jeff to associate director of technology and business development. Now he was flying back and forth every week between FITEL's New York and London offices as he managed the company's 12 programmers and analysts. At the same time, he handled relationships with FITEL's most important clients, such as the investment bank Salomon Brothers. He also managed FITEL people who provided support for customers in North America and as far away as Australia and the Far East.

Responsible for the design, programming, and testing of FITEL's services, Jeff set about improving the firm's computer protocols—that is, the rules that make it possible for one or more computers to communicate with others. The result was that he saved FITEL some 30 percent of its previous cost of communications.

After nearly two years, however, Jeff knew that FITEL was not growing as he had expected. He moved to a job as assistant vice president for Global Fiduciary Services at Bankers Trust Company. The bank handled some $250 billion in pension and profit-sharing plans for more than 100 companies listed in the *Fortune* 500 (an annual list by that magazine of the 500 leading American corporations).

Jeff headed a six-person department that designed a software program that enabled the bank's clients to check the status of their investments at any time. Such a program was a startling innovation in the late 1980s, for bankers were used to distributing, at their convenience, standard printed reports (that is, hard copies) that were produced by their giant mainframe computers. They saw no reason to change. But Jeff, confident in the power of the PC, insisted.

"Jeff sees different ways of doing things and better ways of doing things," a Bankers Trust vice president said later. "He told the naysayers, 'I believe in this new technology and I'm going to show you how it's going to work'—and he did. At the end of the day, he proved them all wrong." The result was that in February 1990 the board of directors of Bankers Trust elected Jeff Bezos as a vice president—the youngest in the bank's history.

Even with the vice presidency, Jeff was already thinking ahead to a different kind of job. He told employment agencies—known as headhunters—he wanted to join a technology company where he could pursue "second phase" automation. He explained this as "the common theme that has run through my life. The first phase of automation is when you use technology to do the same old business processes, but just faster and more efficiently." Point-of-sale systems such as barcode scanners used in grocery stores were examples of the first-phase automation he was describing. The second phase, he said, was "when you can fundamentally change the underlying business process and do things in a completely new way. So it's more of a revolution instead of an evolution."

Probably no one at Bankers Trust knew that the youngest vice president would be the father of a revolution.

3

FATHER OF A REVOLUTION

Jeff had told the headhunters that he did not want to work for another financial company. But one headhunter convinced him he should meet a man named David Shaw, whose firm—D.E. Shaw & Co.—was programming computers to make decisions on when to buy or sell stocks. For example, if the Shaw computer saw that a stock was trading for $199 per share in New York and for $200 a share in London, it would simultaneously buy shares in New York and sell them in London, thus making $1 in profit on each share. *Fortune* magazine called Shaw "the most intriguing and mysterious force on Wall Street."

$1 Million a Year

Jeff met Shaw and they took an immediate liking to each other. Jeff liked the Shaw company's advanced technology, which turned Wall Street thinking upside down. He also liked the fact that the Shaw office had no dress code and no prescribed vacation policy—"You take one when you need one," said Shaw. Jeff remarked that Shaw was "one of those people who has a completely developed left brain and a completely developed right brain. He's artistic, articulate, and analytical. It's just a pleasure to talk to someone like that."

Jeff started work at Shaw in December 1990 as a vice president. Twenty-four months later, when he was 28, he was the company's youngest senior vice president and one of its four managers. Earning more than $1 million a year, he headed a group of 24 employees who worked hard at exploring new business opportunities in a variety of fields ranging from computer software to insurance. In particular, toward the end of 1992, they began to notice something new called the World Wide Web.

At about the same time that year, Jeff and a Shaw employee named MacKenzie Tuttle began to notice each other. A 1992 Princeton graduate, she was a research associate on his staff. In college she had studied creative writing with two prominent novelists and professors: Joyce Carol Oates and Toni Morrison.

Jeff had not had a steady girlfriend since high school. "I didn't really date much until my last year of college," he said. "I had all my friends set me up on blind dates. None

Jeff and Mackenzie Bezos (Associated Press)

of them worked out very well." But when MacKenzie turned up at Shaw, things worked out quite well. She and Jeff were married in 1993.

By the end of that year, the Shaw group was becoming more and more aware of the World Wide Web, which was also becoming known as the Internet. Now David Shaw asked Jeff to explore not just new business opportunities but new *Internet* business opportunities.

Astounding Discovery

Jeff soon learned that use of this thing called the Internet, which almost nobody knew anything about, was growing at the astonishing rate of 2,300 percent a year. "You have to keep in mind," Jeff remarked, "that human beings aren't good at understanding exponential growth. It's just not something we see in our everyday life. But things don't grow this fast outside of petri dishes. It just doesn't happen." In effect, he said, anything growing at such a rate "is invisible today and ubiquitous tomorrow."

Where had the Internet come from? Jeff wondered. The idea, he found, had been born in 1959, some five years before his own birth. The U.S. Department of Defense, challenged by the Soviet Union's launching of its *Sputnik* satellite on October 4, 1957, had decided to create a network of computers. They were programmed to communicate with each other even after a nuclear attack. Developing such a network took 10 years, but in September 1969 a practical system that linked researchers in universities and government agencies began working. It enabled computers in the network to exchange not only data but written messages—the first e-mails.

Following the end of the Cold War in late 1989, the government decided to give up control of its Internet and let businesses not only use it but expand and develop it. By October 1993, a group of University of Illinois students developed the first browser software, called Mosaic. It could retrieve information, including graphics, from anywhere on the Web. Next, the Illinois group created software that could run on Apple's Macintosh and on Microsoft's Windows operating systems. Now the Internet was a practical system connecting computers anywhere and everywhere, and anybody who had a computer was linking to it. The year was 1994 and Jeff Bezos was staring at that incredible, astonishing, staggering figure: growth zooming at 2,300 percent a year. "I'm sitting there," he later recalled, "thinking we can be a complete first mover in e-commerce." E-commerce is business that is handled over the Internet, while an e-business is a business that exists on the Internet. An e-business can buy and sell things by using e-commerce.

Jeff thought about what might be sold on the Internet. For starters, he looked at the mail-order business. He drew up a list of the top 20 things that sold well by mail, ranging from office supplies to music, from clothing to computer software. The more he studied his list, the more *books* moved to its top.

Looking around, Jeff realized that the book business was gigantic but no one dominated it. Among the thousands upon thousands of publishers, not even Random House, the largest, held as much as 10 percent of the total market. Barnes & Noble and the Borders Group, the two largest booksellers, together were selling less than 25 percent of the $30 billion total sales of adult books. And in that year, 1994, customers were expected to buy a total of 513 million books.

No mail-order catalog, Jeff Bezos realized, could contain all the book titles available in any one year. But a computerized catalog could hold millions of titles. The Internet did not care how big a list it was asked to hold.

Exploring the Book Business

Just as Jeff was reviewing the facts and figures about the book business, he realized that the annual convention of the American Booksellers Association was scheduled in Los Angeles over the coming weekend. He flew west.

For three days, Jeff meandered along the convention's aisles. He talked books, book-buying, and bookselling with every representative of every aspect of the business who would talk with him. He learned that two major wholesalers, named Ingram Book Group and Baker & Taylor Books, distributed books to most of the nation's bookstores, acting as the warehouses for them. At their booths, he learned that more data was already available on book titles, authors, and publishers than on almost any other subject or product. The distributors even had CD-ROMs holding the data on some 3 million titles in print. As Jeff later described it, the book business already "had been meticulously organized so it could be put online."

Jeff Bezos returned from Los Angeles convinced that no single bookstore, no matter how gigantic, could hold an

Jeff predicted that the key to a successful high-tech Internet store would be a very low-tech product: books. (Landov)

inventory of the books in print. But an online bookstore could. And the nation's two biggest distributors already had extensive, up-to-the-minute electronic lists. Clearly, the product to sell over the Internet was books.

Now came the biggest surprise. When Jeff told his boss, David Shaw, about the tremendous possibilities of selling books online, Shaw was not interested.

Jeff and MacKenzie talked it over. If the D. E. Shaw firm would not venture into selling books online, what if they did it themselves? MacKenzie agreed. Jeff went back to David Shaw and told him he was going to resign and "do this crazy thing"—sell books on the Internet.

Shaw suggested they take a stroll through New York's Central Park. Over two hours, Shaw talked about his own experience in starting his company, Jeff's importance to the future of D. E. Shaw, and what he would be giving up if he left. Jeff agreed to think it over for another 48 hours.

Jeff thought about the future. He looked ahead, seeing himself as an old man. "I knew that when I was eighty there was no chance that I would regret having walked away from my 1994 Wall Street bonus in the middle of the year," he later said. "But I did think there was a chance that I might regret significantly not participating in this thing called the Internet, that I believed passionately in. I also knew that if I had tried and failed, I wouldn't regret

that. So, once I thought about it that way, it be incredibly easy to make that decision."

Mike and Jackie Bezos, Jeff's parents, were now back in Texas. They got a phone call from Jeff MacKenzie describing their idea of selling books Internet.

"The Internet?" said Mike. "What's that?"

Without hesitating, Jeff's parents offered most c retirement savings—some $300,000—to help laun plan. "We talked about it for two minutes," Jack later. "We didn't invest in Amazon. We invested in

MacKenzie and Jeff called movers to their apartm Manhattan's West Side. They told them to load eve into their truck and head west. They said they wo the movers' headquarters in a couple of days a them just what city to send the truck to.

4

A NEW START IN SEATTLE

In June 1994 Jeff and MacKenzie flew to Fort Worth, Texas, to his parents' home. There Jeff spent a day or two studying the facts on cities in the west. Then he called the movers and told them Seattle, Washington, was their destination. The city boasted hundreds of software companies, from Microsoft and Nintendo to Adobe and RealNetworks, so it had a good pool of computer programming talent. And it was only a six-hour drive from America's largest book distribution center, the Ingram Book Group, in Roseburg, Oregon, so the new Internet bookstore could obtain books for its customers by using same-day or overnight service.

Living in New York, MacKenzie and Jeff had never owned an automobile. Mike Bezos handed Jeff the keys to his six-year-old Chevy Blazer. "This is a car," Jeff later recalled, "that *Consumer Reports* says not to buy used—under _any_ circumstance, at _any_ price. However, they say nothing about accepting one for _free_."

A Is for Amazon

MacKenzie did most of the driving. Jeff sat beside her using his laptop computer to work up a plan for the business. Near the Grand Canyon, they paused while Jeff phoned a Seattle lawyer who had been recommended as an expert in start-up companies. The lawyer asked what the name of the new company was to be. Jeff had thought about that. He wanted a word that had some mystique or charm. "Abracadabra" seemed good, but too long.

"Maybe Cadabra," he told the lawyer.

"Cadaver?" said the lawyer. "Why call your company that?"

Jeff thought some more. Looking for a word that would always appear at or near the top of any list, he read everything under "A" in the dictionary and came up with Amazon—a word high in the alphabet and the name of the river that is 10 times larger than any other. But he insisted that the formal name of his company be Amazon.com. "Everybody thought the '.com' was stupid," a friend later said. "With hindsight, that was brilliant. Today we all talk about '.coms.' Amazon.com was the first. Nobody else was marketing the concept of being a '.com' company. That differentiated Amazon.com in terms of the branding."

Discussing the name, Jeff later said, "It is the right metaphor. People wonder, is it the jungle, the female warriors, or the river? It's the river. Earth's biggest river, earth's biggest selection."

MacKenzie and Jeff did not drive straight to Seattle. They detoured into northern California so Jeff could interview several computer programmers who had been suggested to him. One, who was described by a friend as "a guy who knows how to build very fast databases," was Shel Kaphan. He liked not only Jeff's description of the business he was starting, but also admired Jeff's eager enthusiasm, his hearty laugh, and his disdain for neckties. He agreed to move to Seattle at once.

In Bellevue, a Seattle suburb, the Bezoses rented a three-bedroom ranch house with a garage that had been converted to a family recreation room heated by a pot-bellied stove. Jeff went to Home Depot, bought an inexpensive flush door, some angle irons, and four 4 × 4-inch posts and built a desk. Then he started looking for people to join him and Shel Kaphan.

One who was recommended was Paul Barton-Davis, a programmer in the University of Washington's computer science and engineering department. He later recalled his first visit to the Bezos garage. "Things being very exploratory," he said, "there was nothing in the way of anything actually being set up to do anything. I think there was maybe one SPARCstation [a type of computer server] in there at the time, a desk made out of a door, a bunch of books about business, some stuff from the American Booksellers Association floating around. I wasn't expecting very much, but it was a little bit of a shock."

Nevertheless, Barton-Davis liked what he saw in Jeff Bezos. And Jeff knew that while neither Kaphan nor Barton-Davis had much experience with software for retail business use, they were both extremely smart. He intended to build his business using the smartest people he could find.

Learning the Bookselling Business

Now Jeff knew he had to learn how a book actually gets sold. In September, he spent four days in Portland, Oregon, taking the American Booksellers Association's intensive introductory course in bookselling. There he learned about such matters as managing a store's inventory, ordering and returning books, and developing a business plan. The topic that most interested him, however, was customer service. He took seriously a number of examples of booksellers winning and holding customers by going out of their way to serve them. He returned to Seattle convinced that customer service had to be "the cornerstone of Amazon.com."

Jeff predicted that the key to a successful high-tech Internet store would be a very low-tech product: books. (Landov)

inventory of the books in print. But an online bookstore could. And the nation's two biggest distributors already had extensive, up-to-the-minute electronic lists. Clearly, the product to sell over the Internet was books.

Now came the biggest surprise. When Jeff told his boss, David Shaw, about the tremendous possibilities of selling books online, Shaw was not interested.

Jeff and MacKenzie talked it over. If the D. E. Shaw firm would not venture into selling books online, what if they did it themselves? MacKenzie agreed. Jeff went back to David Shaw and told him he was going to resign and "do this crazy thing"—sell books on the Internet.

Shaw suggested they take a stroll through New York's Central Park. Over two hours, Shaw talked about his own experience in starting his company, Jeff's importance to the future of D. E. Shaw, and what he would be giving up if he left. Jeff agreed to think it over for another 48 hours.

Jeff thought about the future. He looked ahead, seeing himself as an old man. "I knew that when I was eighty there was no chance that I would regret having walked away from my 1994 Wall Street bonus in the middle of the year," he later said. "But I did think there was a chance that I might regret significantly not participating in this thing called the Internet, that I believed passionately in. I also knew that if I had tried and failed, I wouldn't regret that. So, once I thought about it that way, it became incredibly easy to make that decision."

Mike and Jackie Bezos, Jeff's parents, were now living back in Texas. They got a phone call from Jeff and MacKenzie describing their idea of selling books on the Internet.

"The Internet?" said Mike. "What's that?"

Without hesitating, Jeff's parents offered most of their retirement savings—some $300,000—to help launch the plan. "We talked about it for two minutes," Jackie said later. "We didn't invest in Amazon. We invested in Jeff."

MacKenzie and Jeff called movers to their apartment on Manhattan's West Side. They told them to load everything into their truck and head west. They said they would call the movers' headquarters in a couple of days and tell them just what city to send the truck to.

4

A NEW START IN SEATTLE

In June 1994 Jeff and MacKenzie flew to Fort Worth, Texas, to his parents' home. There Jeff spent a day or two studying the facts on cities in the west. Then he called the movers and told them Seattle, Washington, was their destination. The city boasted hundreds of software companies, from Microsoft and Nintendo to Adobe and RealNetworks, so it had a good pool of computer programming talent. And it was only a six-hour drive from America's largest book distribution center, the Ingram Book Group, in Roseburg, Oregon, so the new Internet bookstore could obtain books for its customers by using same-day or overnight service.

Living in New York, MacKenzie and Jeff had never owned an automobile. Mike Bezos handed Jeff the keys to his six-year-old Chevy Blazer. "This is a car," Jeff later recalled, "that *Consumer Reports* says not to buy used—under *any* circumstance, at *any* price. However, they say nothing about accepting one for *free*."

A Is for Amazon

MacKenzie did most of the driving. Jeff sat beside her using his laptop computer to work up a plan for the business. Near the Grand Canyon, they paused while Jeff phoned a Seattle lawyer who had been recommended as an expert in start-up companies. The lawyer asked what the name of the new company was to be. Jeff had thought about that. He wanted a word that had some mystique or charm. "Abracadabra" seemed good, but too long.

"Maybe Cadabra," he told the lawyer.

"Cadaver?" said the lawyer. "Why call your company that?"

Jeff thought some more. Looking for a word that would always appear at or near the top of any list, he read everything under "A" in the dictionary and came up with Amazon—a word high in the alphabet and the name of the river that is 10 times larger than any other. But he insisted that the formal name of his company be Amazon.com. "Everybody thought the '.com' was stupid," a friend later said. "With hindsight, that was brilliant. Today we all talk about '.coms.' Amazon.com was the first. Nobody else was marketing the concept of being a '.com' company. That differentiated Amazon.com in terms of the branding."

Discussing the name, Jeff later said, "It is the right metaphor. People wonder, is it the jungle, the female warriors, or the river? It's the river. Earth's biggest river, earth's biggest selection."

MacKenzie and Jeff did not drive straight to Seattle. They detoured into northern California so Jeff could interview several computer programmers who had been suggested to him. One, who was described by a friend as "a guy who knows how to build very fast databases," was Shel Kaphan. He liked not only Jeff's description of the business he was starting, but also admired Jeff's eager enthusiasm, his hearty laugh, and his disdain for neckties. He agreed to move to Seattle at once.

In Bellevue, a Seattle suburb, the Bezoses rented a three-bedroom ranch house with a garage that had been converted to a family recreation room heated by a pot-bellied stove. Jeff went to Home Depot, bought an inexpensive flush door, some angle irons, and four 4 × 4-inch posts and built a desk. Then he started looking for people to join him and Shel Kaphan.

One who was recommended was Paul Barton-Davis, a programmer in the University of Washington's computer science and engineering department. He later recalled his first visit to the Bezos garage. "Things being very exploratory," he said, "there was nothing in the way of anything actually being set up to do anything. I think there was maybe one SPARCstation [a type of computer server] in there at the time, a desk made out of a door, a bunch of books about business, some stuff from the American Booksellers Association floating around. I wasn't expecting very much, but it was a little bit of a shock."

Nevertheless, Barton-Davis liked what he saw in Jeff Bezos. And Jeff knew that while neither Kaphan nor Barton-Davis had much experience with software for retail business use, they were both extremely smart. He intended to build his business using the smartest people he could find.

Learning the Bookselling Business

Now Jeff knew he had to learn how a book actually gets sold. In September, he spent four days in Portland, Oregon, taking the American Booksellers Association's intensive introductory course in bookselling. There he learned about such matters as managing a store's inventory, ordering and returning books, and developing a business plan. The topic that most interested him, however, was customer service. He took seriously a number of examples of booksellers winning and holding customers by going out of their way to serve them. He returned to Seattle convinced that customer service had to be "the cornerstone of Amazon.com."

Finding Investors and Software

By November 1994, Jeff, MacKenzie, Shel, and Paul were working full time in their cramped garage headquarters. To help make room, they had ripped out the potbellied stove, replacing it with ceramic space heaters. They installed bookshelves, file cabinets, and two computers. They had to step carefully around their garage office, for its floor had become a spaghetti of extension cords.

The men concentrated on designing a database that could store all book orders and customer information. They created the look of the website and developed an e-mail interface to communicate with customers. MacKenzie handled phone calls, ordered materials, and did the bookkeeping and accounting.

During those weeks in the fall of 1994, Jeff Bezos realized he had to solve two problems. One was money. Amazon.com had to be able to pay the people who were getting it going. At the outset, Jeff formed a corporation—that is, a body or organization that is allowed, by the law, to act as if it were a single person. He held several titles in the corporation, including chairman of the board, chief executive officer, president, and founder. For several months, using money he had saved when he was earning $1 million a year on Wall Street, he made loans to the corporation and bought shares of its stock. This ensured his getting his own money back if his company became successful.

Jeff knew he could not go on forever making such loans. He talked up his plans with friends of his parents, classmates and other friends from Princeton, Wall Street buddies, and Seattle investors he had met. With Jeff warning them not to put up the money unless they were willing to risk losing it all, they became the first investors, outside of his family, in his company. Lining them up took several months. Altogether, 62 people were offered the chance to be "angel investors" in Amazon.com. Forty said no. Twenty-two put up about $50,000 apiece, providing a total of $1 million.

The second problem was software. The only software available to manage inventory and process orders was designed for regular mail-order businesses. It could handle just two situations: shipment from available stock, or back-orders (that is, orders that would be filled when stock became available). But Jeff's study of the book business told him that Amazon.com would need to handle many different situations, ranging from shipping available books immediately to shipping out-of-print books when (and if) they could be found in used bookstores.

Shel and Paul went to work developing a software program that could process orders from customers. Finding books by title or author or publisher, handling credit cards, recording the customer's particular interests, recognizing repeat customers, and confirming the shipment of orders were some, but not all, of the many steps the program had to be able to process.

Shel and Paul soon realized how valuable Jeff's own programming experience was. "When Jeff asked, 'can we do this?'" Paul said later, "it was clear that he had already spent a little while in the back of his mind thinking about what might be involved. And he was willing to listen to us in terms of what we should really do about it. He understood the issues involved."

As the months went by, the men developed a catalog of book titles that they estimated would, if printed out, equal seven fat New York City phone books. With their headquarters too cramped for business meetings, they got a kick out of using the Starbucks café in the Barnes & Noble bookstore in downtown Bellevue as their conference room. There MacKenzie interviewed future employees and negotiated business contracts.

By the spring of 1995, Amazon.com totaled five employees (Jeff, MacKenzie, Shel, Paul, and Nicholas Lovejoy, a high school math teacher). To power their computer work stations and equipment and heat the office took lengthy orange extension cords running to the garage from every room in the house, using all available circuit breakers. Housekeeping had to be done with great care, as turning on a vacuum cleaner or hair dryer meant blowing a circuit.

Now came testing. Jeff enlisted dozens of friends, totaling as many as 300, over several weeks in the late spring to use their Internet browsers to search for books on Amazon.com and pretend to buy them. New browsers were almost constantly coming online (Microsoft Internet Explorer, Lynx, and Netscape Navigator arrived in this period), so Jeff and his programmers worked to create a website that was compatible with them all. "We waited until we had the feedback from the test," Barton-Davis said later. "If there was going to be a diversity of browsers, it was much easier testing them with 200 or 300 people than doing it ourselves. By the time we launched the site, we knew that we'd already ironed out 98 percent of the glitches."

Door Desks and Duct Tape

By June, Jeff and his crew were convinced they had all the bugs out of the system. They sent an e-mail to all who had taken part in the test, telling them Amazon.com would open for business on July 6, 1995, and asking them to tell their friends. In the meantime, they rented office space in Seattle's industrial section and moved the Amazon.com headquarters. There they had five rooms on the second floor and, down in the basement, warehouse space about as big as a two-car garage. "For a company that was as high tech and visionary as it was," one of their earliest employees later recalled, "the actual geographical location was a little bit uninspiring. It was a very shabby collection of offices that gave you the impression of being put together with duct tape."

There was one other element in the offices that testified to Jeff Bezos's—and Amazon.com's—sleeves-rolled-up, ready-for-work attitude: Every employee's workstation or desk was a copy of that first one Jeff had built, a simple solid-core door mounted with angle irons on four 4 × 4-inch post legs. Nicholas Lovejoy built four of them for the move from the garage headquarters. The desks were to become a symbol of the company, used in all its offices, as it grew.

Jeff and Shel could not resist rigging their computer workstations to beep each time a sale came in. July 16 brought the first beep. Everyone in the office cheered. But within a week the constant beeping was driving everyone crazy and Shel disconnected the system. Orders totaled more than $12,000 the first week, and nearly $15,000 the next week. During the first month, customers in all 50 states and in 45 countries bought books from Amazon.com. "Within the first few days, I knew this was going to be huge," said Jeff later. "It was obvious that we were onto something much bigger than we ever dared to hope."

Every office employee at Amazon.com has a door desk (like the one pictured here) modeled after the one that Jeff built in his garage office. (Associated Press)

During that summer of 1995, Jeff spent many a long day loading packages of books into the Blazer and delivering them to the post office. By October, orders were flowing in at the rate of 100 a day, and within a year the rate accelerated to 100 per hour. (A rate of 100 every minute was to be commonplace in only a few years.)

No one had expected such a volume of sales. No one had been hired just to pack and ship books. Everyone—all the people MacKenzie and Jeff had interviewed and hired for their bright minds and computer skills—had to pitch in. "We were literally working until midnight every night," Jeff later recalled, "shipping out 100, 200, 300 packages a day. It was backbreaking work. Our knees would be raw." That was because they were packing books on their hands and knees on the concrete floor.

"We've got to get knee pads," said Jeff to Nicholas Lovejoy.

"What about packing tables?" said Lovejoy.

"I thought that was the most brilliant idea I had ever heard in my life," Jeff later said. "It truly dramatically improved things."

Frictionless Shopping in a Clubby Atmosphere

What made Amazon.com such an instant success?

Jeff, Shel, and Paul have long believed that the key to Amazon.com's success is that they worked and experimented for a long time to make the entire Internet shopping process as quick and simple as possible. They called it "frictionless shopping." They made it user-friendly, taking advantage of the Web's ability to search, so their customers could search for any book by title, author, subject, publication date, or keyword. They thought of using the term "Shopping Basket" and made it the standard way for

Internet shoppers to gather their purchases and move to Checkout. And they made it standard practice to confirm every order by e-mail and then e-mail the customer again when the order was shipped.

One of the secrets of Amazon.com's success was price. Regular retail bookstores had to have buildings they built (if they were giant chain stores) or rented from landlords (if they were smaller independent stores). They had to hire salespeople. They had to keep their bookshelves full of inventory. They bought books at a specific discount off the prices marked on them by the publishers—usually paying 60 percent of the retail price, so when they sold the books at full price they could enjoy a 40 percent markup. From that 40 percent they had to pay the rent, employees, light, heat, phone, insurance, advertising, and promotion—and, they hoped, make some profit. Amazon.com, however, had far fewer of such overhead expenses. So the website could price its books lower than most bookstores, passing the discount along to its customers.

Equally as important as such practical matters was the way Amazon.com embraced its customers. It kept track of what books they were buying and recommended similar or related books. Customers who bought a popular book were invited to register to be notified when the author's next book came out. "What hangs it all together," said Paul Barton-Davis, "is that the search language lets you move

queries inside the system. So, when you have just completed a search for something, the system knows. When a customer tells you, 'I'd like to be told about books like this in the future,' the system takes that query and stuffs it away somewhere."

Another unique feature of Amazon.com was that it invited customers to submit their own book reviews and then posted them on the website. This added to the clubby atmosphere, making customers feel they belonged to a special community of book buyers. "We want people to feel like they're visiting a place," said Jeff, "rather than a software application."

While he thought about creating a user-friendly website that was almost a club, Jeff also knew that the competition—the brick-and-mortar stores where customers could see and feel and smell the books and maybe also enjoy a cup of coffee—would wake up any minute and discover what Amazon.com was up to. So his business, he said, would have to work to GET BIG FAST. That phrase became his motto.

Jeff also knew that it would not be easy. This first spurt of growth, he felt, had come because Amazon.com appealed to people who are known in marketing as "early adopters." As he put it, "These were the first people to use computers, to use cell phones. They are the first people to do *everything*."

What his company had to do now, he knew, was get the interest of the ordinary book-buyer who was *not* the first to do everything. "The hardest part with doing something totally new for consumers," he said, "is that they don't adapt to the new habit—no matter how convenient it is. Even if they have Web access on their desk, they don't think about swiveling to their desk and ordering a book. They do what they've always done, which is stop on the way home and buy a book."

Jeff Bezos was determined to make 1996 the year in which Amazon.com did indeed GET BIG FAST.

5

GROWING AND GOING PUBLIC

By December 1995, about 2,200 visitors a day were clicking on the Amazon.com website. The landlord made room for the company to double its office space. More door desks were built for more employees. But by March they had to pack up everything and move to a two-story building that gave them more than eight times as much space plus a big open warehouse area.

Early that spring, Jeff Bezos took a phone call from a stranger who represented a venture-capital fund—that is, a company that specializes in investing in new businesses. Soon after the call, the fund offered to evaluate Amazon. com at $10 million and invest $1 million in it.

Jeff thought about that. He talked with Seattle advisers. "It would be fabulous," said Tom Alberg, a leading Seattle businessman who had been one of the first to recognize the genius of Jeff's Internet plans, "if we could

An Amazon.com warehouse and distribution center
(Associated Press)

get $20 million or $30 million." Stockbroker Eric Dillon, one of Jeff's several mentors who could be depended on for sound advice, said, "If they're willing to give us money, it makes sense to get a *bunch* of money." Jeff waited.

"An underground sensation"

Then came an unexpected boost. On May 16, 1996, a headline on the front page of the *Wall Street Journal* said, "How Wall Street Whiz Found a Niche Selling Books on the Internet." The story told how Amazon.com "has become an underground sensation for thousands of book-lovers around the world, who spend hours perusing its vast electronic library, reading other customers' amusing, online reviews—and ordering piles of books."

The news feature did three things. First, starting on the day it appeared, it doubled Amazon.com's business. "That was a permanent shift," Nicholas Lovejoy said later. "The business kept growing the next day and the next day and the day after that."

Second, the story awakened the competition—namely, Barnes & Noble. The giant bookstore chain went to work designing its own bookselling website.

Third, more venture capital firms knocked on Jeff Bezos's door. Now he was able to get a valuation of $60 million from one called Kleiner Perkins Caufield & Byers. They had invested in large tech companies such as Compaq, Netscape, Intuit, and Sun Microsystems. Putting up $8 million, they became owners of 13 percent of Amazon.com ($8 million is roughly 13 percent of $60 million).

The influx of investment money enabled Jeff to hire needed managers and warehouse workers. By summertime, their building's ground-floor parking garage had become office space. "We're the only start-up company I know that started in a garage," said Jeff, "and then moved to another garage."

One employee, Gina Meyers, who was 40th to join the payroll, later said, "All of the office space was taken up. Nicholas Lovejoy, MacKenzie, me, and one or two temps were in the kitchen area. We just started lining the door desks up. It was very crowded, noisy, and hot."

The *Wall Street Journal* was not the only major publication to tell its readers about Jeff Bezos and his business. Soon *Fortune*, the leading business magazine, ran a major feature story titled "The Next Big Thing: A Bookstore?" And at the end of the year, *Time* magazine cited Amazon.com among the "10 Best Websites of 1996." Favorable publicity, which is always an important element when a new business is getting going, was beginning to come Jeff's way—in a big way.

"Intense, hard-working, smart people"

Everyone in the busy, crowded offices was working long, hard hours to keep up with the demand imposed by eager book-buyers clicking on Amazon.com. And all employees were tuned in to the mindset that Jeff Bezos encouraged with his deep, hearty laugh as, at the first company picnic, he gave each a T-shirt adorned with the motto GET BIG FAST.

Where did Amazon.com people come from? How did Jeff know whom to hire? As his company expanded, he said he looked for "intense, hard-working, smart people" and he wanted them to be so secure themselves that they could "hire other great people. When I interview somebody, I spend about a third of the interview asking them questions designed to ascertain whether or not they can hire great people."

He had something else in mind, too. "When you are working very hard and very long hours," he said, "you want to be around people who are interesting and fun to be with." So he looked for such outside-the-job talent as athletic or musical skills.

"Jeff demanded that you exhibited a track record of success in everything you did," said one associate. "And he demanded that you be smart. He operated on the theory that the best athlete is the smartest athlete. He cared a lot less about relevant experience—because there wasn't any relevant experience—and a lot more about people who demonstrated a track record of being super smart."

One of Jeff's Princeton classmates, David Risher, who became a senior vice president at Amazon.com, recalled how Jeff interviewed job applicants—a task Jeff kept for himself until the company got too big early in 1997. After talking with them about their personal hobbies and pastimes and their values, said Risher, Jeff would pop unexpected questions at them. Typical was "How would you design a car for a deaf person?"

"The best candidates," Risher recalled, "say they'd plug their ears and drive around in their cars to experience what it feels like to be a deaf driver. They put themselves right into the customer's mind and body, to find out what they need." Applicants who could think that way, and who showed that they wanted to have a voice in Amazon.com's intense, hard-working culture, usually were hired.

Jeff had his own way of describing the atmosphere or culture he wanted Amazon.com to have for its employees. He said he expected it to be "intense and friendly," adding that, "if you ever have to give up 'friendly' in order to have 'intense,' we would do that."

One employee remembered what she saw when she went for her first interview. "People were dashing back and forth," she said. "There was a huge sense of cama-raderie. Construction people were bringing in desks and computers. It was total mayhem. I thought, 'This is great. I want to work here.'"

Jeff knew that, intense as the office atmosphere was, it was the distribution warehouse that made Amazon.com successful. He often reminded warehouse workers that their customers knew only two things about the company: the website and the books they ordered and received. He visited the warehouse often, pitching in to help sort books and pack them.

The original warehouse group was a colorful bunch sent in by agencies for temporary employees. Students, musicians, and computer geeks, they were young and full of energy and wore a rainbow of hair colors. By midsummer 1996, they had fully bonded. "We were the core," said one. "We *were* Amazon."

They showed that spirit that July when Jeff made one of his warehouse visits. Immediately, several workers began firing rubber bands at the boss. Without hesitation, he grabbed rubber bands from the floor and started shooting back. "I will say this about Jeff Bezos," said one later, "I would want him on my side in a rubber-band war."

The year 1996 was a pivotal one for Jeff Bezos and Amazon.com. In March the company had moved to its two-story building. By mid-summer the building was jammed with people, so in August that office was made into the warehouse, and the management people moved two miles away. By November the warehouse had outgrown the two-story building, so the entire distribution operation moved into 93,000 square feet of space on Dawson Street. "It was so big," said one long-time warehouse worker, "it was like being out in the country—you couldn't see your neighbor. We figured we would last there for years. Three months later we were elbow to elbow."

A simple fact explains that growth. In July 1996, Amazon.com was ordering 100 books a day from the leading distributors—Ingram and Baker & Taylor—and directly from publishers. By December, it was ordering 5,000 books a day.

Another important element of Amazon.com emerged in 1996. That summer, a customer asked if it was all right for her to link her website, on which she recommended books, to Amazon.com. Jeff said yes and the company set up a network of Amazon Associates, which now includes hundreds of sites. A visitor to any site on any subject can click directly to Amazon.com's database on the subject and find related recommendations and book reviews. The original site's owner gets a commission of 5 to 15 percent of the price of any book Amazon sells that way.

Amazon.com Goes Public

In the first three months of 1997, Jeff Bezos was, as usual, keeping a close watch on his company's sales. Amazon .com's database now included 340,000 customers in more than 100 countries. Forty percent of them were repeat customers. By March, average daily visits to the website were 80,000, up from 2,200 in December 1995. Total sales for those first three 1997 months were $16 million—more than all 1996 sales. Yet the company was losing money because Jeff and his people did not insist on making a profit. Rather, they were making their business grow by offering discounts and spending money to develop and promote their website. The company lost $2.97 million in the first three months of 1997, with $9 million lost altogether since it started. Nevertheless, it was time, Jeff knew, to go public.

When a company "goes public," it invites any and all investors who may be interested to buy shares of stock in the company. It begins by making an initial public offering (IPO) of a certain number of shares—usually at least a million—at a certain price each. The IPO is usually made by an investment bank—a firm that specializes in underwriting IPOs. The underwriter guarantees that it will buy the shares at the fixed price on the fixed date and in turn sell them to the public.

In December 1996 Jeff had hired 33-year-old Joy Covey to be Amazon.com's chief financial officer and vice president of finance and administration. She had become a certified public accountant at 19 and had earned degrees in both business and law at Harvard in 1990. With a brilliant background in software and digital companies, she was one more example of Jeff's philosophy of finding the smartest people for Amazon.com. "Nobody is as quick as Joy," said Nicholas Lovejoy. "On her second day, she cornered me and Shel and spent three hours to have us overview the entire system. She asked great questions. She understood every bit of it. She can cope with incredible volumes of information in incredibly short order."

Joy Covey got eight leading investment banks that specialized in technology companies to make proposals on how they would handle the Amazon.com IPO. The Deutsche Morgan Grenfell (DMG) bank won. She and Jeff flew to Europe. Over only three days in Zurich, Geneva, Paris, and London, they presented the Amazon.com story to five investor meetings a day. Back in the United States, they visited 20 cities, making 48 presentations in 16 days.

Time and again, they made it clear that Amazon.com was different. "The Company believes," said the plan they presented, "that it will incur substantial operating losses for the foreseeable future, and that the rate at which such losses will be incurred will increase significantly from current levels." In other words, they warned investors that Amazon.com was not a profitable operation even though it intended to be one someday. Home again and exhausted, they were confident that the investment world understood their business and its future.

On May 15, 1997, Jeff's company went public at $18 per share, with 3 million shares available. At age 33, holding

Joy Covey (center) is Amazon.com's chief financial officer. She is pictured here with two executives of the Chicago Board Options Exchange. (Associated Press/Chicago Board Options Exchange)

9.88 million shares, his worth on paper was $177.8 million. The annual salary he was letting his company pay him was $64,333. He himself owned 42 percent of the company, and close family members held another 10 percent. That meant that 52 percent of the voting power of the company was held by the Bezos family. (Incidentally, the investment that venture-fund capitalists Kleiner

Perkins Caufield & Byers had made in 1996 proved profitable, as the IPO gained them 3 million shares.)

They all had something else to think about, however. Three days before the IPO, a lawsuit against Amazon.com had been filed in federal court in Manhattan.

6

GETTING BIGGER FASTER

The lawsuit was brought by Barnes & Noble. It charged that Amazon.com was making a false claim on its website and in its advertising. The claim was that Amazon.com was "Earth's Biggest Bookstore." According to Barnes & Noble, Amazon.com was not "a bookstore at all. It is a book broker making use of the Internet exclusively to generate sales to the public."

Another false claim, said Barnes & Noble, was that Amazon.com "offers over one million titles, more than five times as many titles as you'll find in even the largest Barnes & Noble." On the contrary, the suit said, "Amazon's warehouse in Seattle stocks only a few hundred titles. Barnes & Noble stocks more books than Amazon and there is no book that Amazon can obtain which Barnes & Noble cannot."

Barnes & Noble also insisted that on January 28, 1997, it had demanded "that Amazon cease and desist from making these false and misleading claims. To date Amazon has refused to do so." Now the bookstore was asking a federal court to order Amazon.com to stop running its advertising and publish "corrective" ads. And Barnes & Noble was ready to make its own claim as "The World's Largest Bookseller Online."

Some experts thought the lawsuit marked the beginning of the end for Amazon.com. One prominent Wall Street researcher compared the two companies and remarked, "Amazon.*toast*." An article in *Fortune*, the leading authority among magazines about business, was headlined, "Why Barnes & Noble May Crush Amazon.com." A price war broke out online, with Barnes & Noble customers getting 20 percent off paperbacks and 30 percent off hardcovers, and Amazon.com customers getting similar discounts plus 40 percent off some books.

Jeff Bezos relished the battle. "We've always offered the biggest selection," he announced, "and with these prices Amazon.com offers the lowest everyday book prices anywhere in the world—online or off." He had long ago decided, he said, to match the power of Barnes & Noble. That was the aim of his GET BIG FAST strategy.

By August, Amazon.com was in the courts with a countersuit. It charged that Barnes & Noble was engaging in unfair competition by not adding sales taxes to the prices of books it sold on its website. Amazon.com's argument pointed out that companies selling by mail order were required to charge sales tax to those customers who lived in the states where the companies had stores, but they did not have to make out-of-state customers pay sales taxes. Therefore, claimed Amazon.com, Barnes & Noble should be required to add sales tax to every Internet order in each of the 48 states where it maintained stores. Otherwise, said the lawsuit, Barnes & Noble had an "unlawful advantage" over Amazon.com because it was "able to charge significantly less than required by law."

The court battle ended in October with an out-of-court settlement. Neither side paid any damages or admitted doing anything wrong. Both declared they "simply decided that they would rather compete in the marketplace than in the courtroom."

Patenting the System and Capturing the Flag

While all this was going on, Jeff and his programmers were as busy as ever making improvements on their website. One of the most valuable—to customers and to Amazon.com—was its "1-Click" technology, first installed in September 1997. If you were a new customer, it securely recorded all your information—name, address, book interests, billing and shipping information—so that the next time you went to Amazon.com it recognized you and you did not have to do anything other than click in. The system was so new and different that Amazon.com filed for a U.S. patent on it.

One prominent visitor to the Seattle headquarters provided a highlight in the fall of 1997. On the Amazon.com website, a time line of the company history noted his visit: "November. Vice President Al Gore drops by. Works customer service phone queues. Looks spiffy in headset. Doesn't do a bad job, at all." That time line message, many agreed, read just the way Jeff Bezos talked.

As the year ended, Jeff's company was growing at a rate of 3,000 percent—even faster than the Internet's 2,300 percent growth rate that had first attracted Jeff. Sales for the year reached $147 million.

Walkie-Talkie Radios, Night-Vision Goggles, Shelebration

Jeff and MacKenzie headed for a Christmas visit with his family, who were now living on Amelia Island, Florida. They gave his parents and brother and sister laser-tag guns and vests, while his parents gave everyone walkie-talkie radios. Using them, all zapped each other during nighttime games of Capture the Flag and took the fun with them—pretending to be Navy SEALs—when they had to shop for milk late at night. "I never realized my mother was such a good shot," said Jeff later. His mother, however, unhappily discovered that Jeff played the game wearing night-vision goggles MacKenzie supplied. Jeff, laughing his lovable, hearty guffaw, replied, "It's not clear that you're supposed to have a level playing field when you're marching into battle."

The year 1998 brought even more growth at Amazon.com, but with some ups and downs. Jeff and all other Amazon.com stockholders saw the price per share go from $40 in May to $140 in July, and then down to $70 in August. The stock was split twice during the year. A stock split means that an investor automatically gets two more shares for each one that he or she owns. At the same time, each share's price is divided by three. So, after a split, a stock that cost $33 per share looked like a bargain compared to the same stock when it cost $100 per share before the split. Investors, who were eagerly riding the crest of the rolling wave of high-technology stocks, happily bought stock in Amazon.com.

It was time to branch out from books. In June, Amazon.com announced it was ready to ship music CDs. Jeff and his associates had worked out a system that offered customers about 10 times the selection they would see in any music store, at half the music-store prices. By October, nobody had to say GET BIG FAST about the music business—Amazon.com was the biggest seller of music online. Customers could listen to samples of more than 225,000 recordings and click onto critical reviews or educational information about musicians or types of music. Jeff called the site "not just a store—it's a place where you can learn about music."

Jeff followed up that thought by launching Amazon.com's Advantage for Music program. This enabled independent musicians and small businesses that produced records to sell their CDs on Amazon.com alongside the major record companies. The result was that tens of thousands of independent musical artists have been able to sell their music to millions of buyers.

Selling music was a first step in a plan Jeff had recently described. "Our strategy is to become an electronic commerce destination," he had said a few months earlier. "When somebody thinks about buying something online, even if it is something we do not carry, we want them to come to us. We would like to make it easier for people online to find and discover the things they might want to buy online, even if we are not the ones selling them."

A month after Amazon.com started selling music CDs, Jeff had an idea that added yet more pizzazz to his website. It was an addition to the regular book listings that ranked the books according to their sales over the preceding 24 hours. The rankings, in fact, would change every hour—a feat that only the well-programmed computer could accomplish. Amazon.com employees, almost every one, thought it was a senseless idea. "We can do it in 48 hours," said Jeff. "I want it done. Let's do it."

The rankings idea proved to Jeff's people that he had an uncanny ability to come up with notions that were extremely helpful to the growth of their business. Authors wrote colorful essays for the op-ed pages of the *New York Times* and *Wall Street Journal* arguing for and against the rankings. The publicity rippled along to Internet users everywhere, giving even more reasons for checking into Amazon.com.

August 1998 marked the fourth anniversary of Shel Kaphan's starting work on Amazon.com in the Bezos garage. Jeff decided the event called for what he announced would be a "Shelebration." He told all members of the Amazon.com engineering staff to pack their bags, gather their spouses, and report to the Seattle airport. Off they all went, including Jeff and MacKenzie, on a chartered airplane to Hawaii. When they reached a house that Jeff had rented, they were welcomed by an even larger group that had arrived first: a bunch of Shel's old friends from San Francisco, for whom Jeff had chartered a plane from San Jose.

The Shelebration was typical of Jeff's way of doing things. It brought to life the business philosophy he often expressed in the words: "Work Hard, Have Fun, Make History."

Another example of Jeff's relaxed relationship with his employees was Amazon.com's purchase that August of a company called Junglee. Based in Silicon Valley (the area around San Jose where countless computer technology

Jeff has always planned for Amazon.com to GET BIG FAST by selling anything anyone could want. Here he is pictured riding a Segway Human Transporter, for which Amazon.com was the first vendor. Behind him is Segway inventor and chairman Dean Kamen. (Landov)

companies have been born), it produced a shopping guide that used software that enabled Web shoppers to compare products they were thinking about buying.

Back in April, Jeff's company treasurer, Randy Tinsley, had recommended that Amazon.com buy the Junglee company. He and Jeff had debated the idea for half an hour, with Tinsley thinking that the Junglee people might not want to sell their business. Finally, Jeff had ended the discussion, saying, "We have a million other things to do. Drop it." But within two hours Tinsley told Jeff that he had gone ahead and called Junglee and guess what? They were interested. "It shows you," said Jeff, laughing his deep, powerful laugh, "how much people listen to me."

Expanding to Europe

Selling music CDs and providing a way for customers to comparison shop were just two steps in the growing progress of Jeff's GET BIG FAST plan. The fall of 1998 brought several more steps. In October, Jeff announced that customers in Germany could now get Amazon.com's services by clicking on Amazon.de, for Amazon.com had bought Germany's online bookstore, Telebuch. It listed 400,000 German-language titles. That same month, customers in the United Kingdom could find all 1.2 million books in print in Britain by going to Amazon.co.uk. Jeff had bought up that country's electronic bookstore, called Bookpages. Distribution was centered in warehouses in Regensburg, Germany, and Slough, England.

An interviewer later wondered if sales in foreign countries would compete with selling books here in America. "Most of our growth outside of the U.S.," Jeff replied, "comes from local operations." For example, he said, "In Germany most of our sales are in German books, and most of those books don't have to move across borders." He added that sales in other countries were now totaling about one fourth of all Amazon.com business.

The *Harry Potter* books gave Amazon.com and Amazon.co.uk a problem that year. The first book, *Harry Potter and the Sorcerer's Stone*, had been a huge success in America. Now came the second, *Harry Potter and the Chamber of Secrets*. But it was published in Britain several months before its scheduled publication in the United States. So, of course, American fans of Harry Potter did not want to wait—they were eager to order the latest book from England. Amazon.com obliged by building up anticipation with about 80 enthusiastic reviews and offering directions on how to order the book from Amazon.co.uk for about $23 in American money. Delivery took only eight days.

The situation angered the American publishers of the *Harry Potter* books because they were sure that Amazon.com was taking sales away from them and giving them to the British publishers. It took sensitive negotiations to settle the dispute, with Jeff Bezos's people pointing out that Amazon.com had been selling books all over the world since its first month in business. International sales were as much a part of the Internet as international information.

At about this time in 1998, Jeff had a chance to tell people about the international aspects of Amazon.com's business. In one of the public speeches he was now often making, he talked about doing business with customers who had long been oppressed in countries that were in the Soviet bloc. "People will go to great lengths," he said, "because they want access to information and things that help them educate themselves." Then he described an Amazon.com order from a Romanian customer who had no credit card. The order included a floppy disk in its own sleeve. Written on the sleeve was the message, "The customs inspectors steal the money, but they don't read English. It's inside the floppy disk." Concealed inside the sleeve were two folded $100 bills.

Those who knew Jeff well were not surprised when they heard about how he handled the expansion into Germany. The head of Germany's largest media company, Bertelsmann AG, had been determined to own half of Amazon.com. He insisted on holding meetings with Jeff, making offers that he may have thought were irresistible. At one point, learning that Jeff and MacKenzie were on vacation in Turkey, he sent his company's corporate jet to fly them to a meeting in Germany. But after long discussions in four such meetings, Jeff said no. "Jeff made the decision not to do it," his mentor Tom Alberg said later, "based on thinking we could do it as well on our own."

The German experience proved that while Jeff Bezos was not about to let any giant corporation buy his company, he was quite capable of helping his company grow by buying others.

The Place to Find Anything You Want Online

Customers who checked the Amazon.com time line in November discovered an engaging, Jeff-like message: "We're ready for our closeup, Mr. DeMille: Amazon.com's Video & DVD store opens." By December the Junglee shopping guide site had a new name: Amazon.com's "Shop the Web." Its home page described it as "the place to find anything you want to buy on line." Clicking on links took customers directly to such retail stores as Cyberian Outpost for computers, Gap for clothing, or a range of products from toys to travel arrangements.

When their business grew out of its garage beginnings, Jeff and MacKenzie Bezos had rented a small apartment in downtown Seattle that was within walking distance of their office. Only now did they buy their own home—a big, five-bedroom, $10-million house in Seattle's exclusive suburb, Medina. Their friends knew that such an expenditure was rare for the Bezoses, even though Jeff's net worth, which any person who followed the stock market could guess, was about $10 billion. And, characteristically, his car was a basic Honda Accord.

By the last month of 1998, Jeff Bezos had approved the creation of five new giant warehouse distribution centers to be opened in 1999. They were networked to the established Seattle warehouse and to one in Delaware that had been set up a year or so earlier to give fast service to customers in the eastern states. Located in North Dakota, Nevada, Kentucky, Georgia, and Kansas, the new warehouses were mostly in states that, like Delaware, did not have to add sales taxes to in-state purchases. From them, merchandise could be sent directly—usually overnight or within two days—to customers.

Building the warehouses cost $200 million. Designed especially for Amazon.com's unique system of filling Internet orders, they covered 3 million square feet altogether. Jeff estimated that they would give him enough space to handle $15 billion in sales every year.

The 1998 Christmas season proved that Jeff Bezos had been right when he predicted that people would buy on the Internet not only books but countless other items they usually bought in retail stores. Altogether, Internet sales totaled more than $3.5 billion. Amazon.com itself counted up more than 9 million individual visitors to its website.

The holiday season proved to be no holiday for Amazon.com employees. "At Christmas," recalled one warehouse worker afterward, "everybody had to come to the warehouse and work elbow to elbow. They would rotate in people from the corporate offices when we didn't have enough staff. There would be times when Jeff Bezos, Joy Covey, customer service, vice presidents, and the marketing department would help gift wrap, push boxes, and pick orders. So there was a lot of impromptu training. It did promote a feeling of camaraderie."

With his sleeves rolled up, Jeff was at the heart of the busy operation. When the season was over, the accounting reports proved that "Work Hard, Have Fun, Make History" was not an idle motto. Having fun during their hard-working camaraderie, the Amazon.com crew had indeed made history: In the holiday season from November 17 to December 31, 1.7 million new customers had become Amazon.com fans. Some 7.5 million items had been shipped to new and old customers, and total sales had mounted to almost $253 million. And for the total year, book sales alone had reached $610 million—313 percent more than 1997's $147.8 million.

Meantime, in mid-December, people who owned stock in Amazon.com again saw its worth zoom up and down. The price per share on the morning of December 15 was $243. By noontime, it was higher than $300. At the day's end, it was $259. The company's market value—that is, the price at which buyers and sellers would agree to do business—had shot up higher than that of such respected companies as International Paper, Alcoa, and Caterpillar.

Amazon.com employees filling last-minute orders during a busy Christmas season (Associated Press)

Just three and a half years after Jeff Bezos invited 300 friends and family members to try out his crazy idea, his brainchild was the third largest bookseller in America. Only the bookstore chains Barnes & Noble and Borders were larger. And GET BIG FAST were still the three most important words in Jeff's vocabulary.

7

"SOMETHING THE WORLD HAS NEVER SEEN"

As 1999 began, business experts were predicting that in the coming year more than 10 million customers could be expected to buy their books, CDs, and other items—worth some $1.4 billion altogether—through Jeff Bezos's company. Looking to the future, Jeff's mentor Tom Alberg said, "Jeff has the capability of creating a Microsoft, a General Electric, a Wal-Mart." Jeff himself said, "We want to build something the world has never seen."

The Secrets of Success

Jeff thought about what had made Amazon.com so successful. "The Internet is this big, huge hurricane," he remarked. "The only constant in that storm is the customers." Service to customers, he was convinced, was the secret. Amazon.com had made it possible for customers to go to a single site and find any book they wanted—or discover a book they did not know they wanted—and buy it immediately with a single click of the mouse. Amazon.com had also known how to hug its customers, including them in the family by inviting them not only to read book reviews but to write them—even negative ones. It knew how to greet customers who came back, treating them as old friends by remembering their interests and tastes. And it knew how to use e-mail to cement a friendship.

Thinking about all that, Jeff commented early in 1999: "When we first started Amazon.com, we had very conscious discussions where we talked about the fact that we were not a bookstore, but we were a book service. I do think that is a better way to think about it. Thinking of yourself as a store is too limiting. Services can be anything."

Jeff also considered some key facts about selling on the Internet. One was that, because the Internet was the World Wide Web (www) that could be reached by any computer anywhere, an Internet business was automatically global the day it started. Another fact was that it needed no infrastructure, that is, the things that would go along with operating a brick-and-mortar bookstore, such as a building and bookshelves. Third, it could provide better service than

any store in a shopping plaza or mall. Fourth, any kind of product could be available on what Jeff was beginning to think of as a "cyberstore." And fifth, investors were attracted to providing capital money to help launch and sustain Internet stores. Amazon.com itself was now worth $32 billion while investment in such stores as Sears and Kmart together now totaled $17 billion.

"Our vision," Jeff concluded, "is the world's most customer-centric company. The place where people come to find and discover anything they might want to buy online." Amazon.com's goal, he said, was not to be "Earth's biggest bookstore" but "Earth's biggest anything store."

As he encouraged Amazon.com's employees to think of "Earth's biggest anything store," Jeff kept reminding them of what he called the company's Six Core Values. They were:

1. Customer obsession. Serving the customer—providing what the customer wanted at the lowest possible price and at the fastest possible speed—was always the most important job.
2. Ownership. Every employee was offered the opportunity to be a stockholder in Amazon.com. "Everyone," said Jeff, "is an owner."
3. Bias for action. "Do it now." "Don't procrastinate." "Make it happen." Those were Jeff Bezos's kinds of phrases—plus, of course, GET BIG FAST.

4. Frugality. Big and successful as Amazon.com was, every desk or work station was a door with 4 × 4-inch post legs attached with angle irons. Money was not spent on decor or luxuries.

5. High hiring bar. Amazon.com still wanted smart people. It sifted through resumes and interviews to find them.

6. Innovation. Amazon.com continued to introduce new ideas, new systems, and new offerings to customers.

From Auctions to E-cards

Business experts saw one Amazon.com innovation after another in 1999. In February, the Bezos company bought 46 percent of drugstore.com, giving Amazon.com customers an efficient way to buy health-care products online. March brought the announcement of an auction site on Amazon.com ready to compete with eBay. It was designed to help customers find anything they wanted, either through any store or any individual. "You realize very quickly," said Jeff, "that you can't sell everything people might want directly. So instead you need to do that in partnership with thousands and indeed millions of third-party sellers in different ways."

To launch that site, Amazon.com auctioned off a number of collectors' items for the benefit of the World Wildlife

Fund, devoting the proceeds to the preservation of South America's Amazon rain forest. One item offered was Jeff's original $60 door desk. His mother bought it when the auction bidding reached $30,100.

Next, in March, Amazon.com bought 50 percent of Pets.com, a small online company in California, so its customers could buy their pet foods and accessories on their favorite website. Starting in April, they could send greeting cards free of charge from Amazon.com Cards. With 45 subject categories, it let customers choose from some 800 different e-cards. That offering, said Jeff, was "based on the belief that if cards were free the world would be a better place."

The good publicity continued that spring. On March 25, the *Wall Street Journal* saluted Joy Covey, Amazon's chief financial officer. She had been traveling across America to meet with investors and people who analyzed stocks, working to convince them that the company's giant sales and unprofitable operation would, in the future, mean even bigger sales and real profits. Almost at the same time, *Forbes* magazine (another business magazine that is a strong competitor to *Fortune*) published a major feature on Joy. And later, in September, *Fortune* said Joy Covey was the 28th most powerful woman in American business, crediting her with "convincing Wall Street that a profitless company was worth $22 billion."

By July, Amazon.com had served its 10-millionth customer. Now it began selling toys. Its time-line page again sounded like Jeff speaking: "Amazon.com Toys opens for business. Customers' Slinky needs, thankfully, are met."

That July brought supportive comments from the publisher of *Forbes* magazine, Rich Karlgaard. Writing in the *Wall Street Journal*, he said that Amazon.com was "bulletproof evidence that we live in a New Economy." Karlgaard went even further in his own column in *Forbes*. "Amazon is the first shining ray of the new commercial millennium pure Web play," he said, "fleeting as a shooting star, unburdened by any legacy baggage at all. It's the shape of business in the next century."

A Patent on a Discussion

On August 2, 1999, the United States Patent and Trademark Office in Washington received a patent application from Jeffrey P. Bezos of Seattle. While any patent application is for an invention that is unusual, this one was more unusual than most: The invention was, in effect, a conversation. The abstract of the application—that is, the summary describing what the invention was—said that Mr. Bezos wanted to patent "a method and system for conducting an electronic discussion relating to a topic."

The abstract said that the discussion system receives an item to be the topic of the discussion and then receives comments related to the item and sends a message that describes it and the comments received. It next sends all that to participants in the discussion and gets back more comments to add to the original message. Finally, it sends all that once more to all participants.

In effect, Jeff wanted to patent the process that he had invented in 1995 to make Amazon.com's website work. The application included several pages of detailed text, plus 13 drawings (with a detailed text description of each). It also had a long list of other patents that served as background to this invention, and a list of 71 "claims"—that is, reasons why this system was unique and should be granted a patent.

Why did Jeff want a patent on the Amazon.com system? Because a patent could keep other businesses from making, using, or selling his invention. If it were patented, others would have to be licensed—that is, they would have to buy permission—to use it. In fact, Jeff had just received a patent on his 1-Click ordering operation. Now he wanted to prove ownership of the full system that enabled customers worldwide to participate in Amazon.com's unique website.

That October, in fact, Amazon.com sued Barnesandnoble .com over the 1-Click ordering process, claiming that the bookstore's website copied Amazon.com's. Amazon.com won on December 2 when a court order, called a temporary injunction, forced Barnesandnoble.com to stop using the process.

Jeff held other patents, too. Four were for search engines he had invented to make the Amazon.com website work quickly and easily. Another was for the exclusive secure server the site used.

November brought a major press conference in New York City with Jeff at center stage. "Sixteen months ago," he said, "Amazon.com was a place where you could find books. Tomorrow, Amazon.com will be a place where you can find anything, with a capital A."

He was officially opening zShops, the new "online mall" of Amazon.com. On it, for a monthly fee of only $9.99 plus a commission paid to zShops, any small business could sell almost anything to anybody. The idea was like the original Amazon.com concept of selling books by listing many thousand titles but not actually maintaining an inventory of them. zShops could list more than half a million products—far more than even the largest Wal-Mart or Target store could hold—and the individual small shops would fill the orders.

With the end-of-year holiday shopping season coming, Jeff spread the radius of Amazon.com's circle of customer services even more widely. By the end of November, the website's visitors could buy tools and hardware, video games and computer software, leather goods, and jewelry. They could also sign up for the site's own credit card, which was expected to add $30 million a year in fees to Amazon.com's income.

Promising a Profit

Four times a year, Jeff Bezos invited all Amazon.com workers in Seattle to what he called an "all hands" meeting. As the end of 1999 drew near, some 2,000 employees packed into a giant hotel ballroom. They heard their boss review the status of books, music, and videos—the three basic products on which their business had been built.

Most Amazon.com workers knew that the company had never declared a profit. Jeff and his advisers had steadily used whatever was earned from sales to expand their business. That was how—in 1999 alone—they had bought up nine smaller Internet companies, opened seven new online stores, and built five huge warehouse distribution centers. They had concentrated on investing in new and wider markets that totaled 13 million customers rather than on declaring profits that Wall Street could applaud. They had done what was commonly known as "plowing the profits back into the business."

Now all hands heard Jeff announce that "by the end of the year 2000" Amazon.com's sales of books, music, and videos would be a profitable operation. Stunned, his 2,000 people sat in silence. Jeff grinned. "You can cheer," he

Jeff was named Time *magazine's Person of the Year in December 1999.* (Time Life Pictures)

said. They cheered. That December, Amazon.com shipped more than 20 million items.

December brought a different kind of announcement from a different source. *Time* magazine's December 27 cover story revealed that its editors had elected Jeff Bezos as *Time's* Person of the Year. At 35, he was the fourth youngest person ever to win the honor. Previous recipients of the award included 25-year-old Charles A. Lindbergh in 1927, for his solo flight across the Atlantic Ocean; 26-year-old Queen Elizabeth II in 1952, for her succession to the throne of England and the United Kingdom; and 34-year-old Martin Luther King Jr. in 1963, for his leadership of the civil rights movement.

8

KING OF CYBERCOMMERCE

The editors of *Time* devoted 33 pages to the story of Amazon.com's Jeff Bezos and Internet shopping. They said Jeff was "unquestionably the king of cybercommerce" and that he had "helped build the foundation of our future." Editor James Kelly wrote: "He has helped guarantee that the world of buying and selling will never be the same."

Jeff maintained his self-confidence and kept his ego from swelling. "This is an incredible and humbling honor," he said. "The Internet holds the promise to improve lives and empower people. I feel very lucky to be involved in this time of rapid and amazing change."

Describing Jeff's achievement as the result of planning and hard work rather than luck, *Time* said, "Bezos & Co. conceived an entirely new way of thinking about the ancient art of retailing, from creating a 'flow experience' that keeps customers coming back to Amazon's website to read product reviews or one another's 'wish lists,' to automating as much as possible a complex process that starts when you hit the patent-protected '1-Click' buy technology and ends when your purchase is delivered to your door." The magazine quoted an investment executive: "Wall Street will look back and realize management's foresight in developing one of the smartest strategies in business history."

As 1999 ended, Amazon.com's stock price soared again, reaching $94 per share. Jeff's shares—on paper—were valued at $10.5 billion. He had already sold off enough shares to provide about $25 million in cash, which enabled MacKenzie and him to buy their home and secure their own future. And their future now included the expected arrival of their first child in March 2000.

Hi-tech Bubble Bursts

The new year, however, brought major changes. For nearly 10 years, investors in high technology companies had seen their companies' stocks grow and grow. Now that "bubble" was bursting. In January, stock in Amazon.com lost 40 percent of its value. The customers of "Earth's biggest anything store" were spending less. For the first time, Jeff and his managers had to lay off some employees—1,300 altogether. Jeff made sure that company stock worth $2.5 million was set aside for them.

There were other problems, too. Jeff and his company had to face some setbacks. Investing in Pets.com proved to be a mistake, as did Amazon.com's attempt to sell furniture online with Living.com. "I could have saved significant sums of money," Jeff later remarked, "but when you're building a company you're going to make some bets that are going to end up well, and other bets that aren't good. If you don't take those risks, you'll lose out to the companies that do."

MacKenzie's and Jeff's son, Preston Bezos, was born in March. A delighted father, Jeff took to interrupted sleep and changing diapers as if they were the best things that ever happened to him. In public he announced that he wished, now that he could understand what his mother had done for him, he had treated her better when he was a teenager.

Growing in New Directions

Despite the bursting bubble of the hi-tech world, Jeff kept pushing for Amazon.com to expand. In April 2000, as homeowners' thoughts turned to the outdoors, he added a new store for patio furniture. In May he entertained reporters in New York by appearing in a chef's apron and hat to announce, along with the well-known Martha

Stewart, that Amazon Kitchen was open for business. It offered Internet shoppers a wide assortment of cooking materials: utensils, recipes, accessories, and tips from Martha herself.

By summertime, Amazon.co.jp had opened in Japan and Amazon.fr was serving the French. Jeff now made a deal with Toysrus.com, which had its own online store, to create a giant store using both names. With his worldwide staff totaling some 7,000, he needed more people despite the layoffs back in January. A reporter asked if it was hard to attract and keep employees when the Amazon.com stock price was sinking. "Of course, smart employees always want to join when the stock is down," Jeff answered, "and since we don't want any dumb employees, it works out pretty well."

Concluding that reporter's interview, Jeff said, "We are at the tip of the iceberg. It's hard for people to imagine just how good e-commerce is going to be ten years from now."

As 2001 began, Jeff looked at Amazon.com's problems and progress. A year ago, its stock had reached a high of $106 per share. Now it was down at $15.60. But, as always, Jeff did not worry about the company stock price, for he knew that Amazon.com had served 20 million customers in 2000—and that was 6 million more than in 1999. Sales for the year had grown from 1999's $1.64 billion to $2.76 billion for 2000. Overall, his company was still not making

Amazon.com has opened Internet stores in countries around the world. Here Jeff is pictured with Junichi Hasegawa, country manager for Japan's Amazon.co.jp. (Getty Images North America)

a profit, but Jeff was confident that its persistent growth promised Amazon.com's workers and stockholders a bright future.

Jeff continued to amuse and astonish his Internet customers. Amazon.co.jp was adding videos and CDs to its Internet offerings, so as a crowd of 350 journalists watched, Jeff Bezos—wearing the uniform of a delivery person from Nippon Express—delivered a Japanese family's first order. To the delight of Amazon.com's publicity people, the videotape of the delivery was played again and again on Japanese television.

Obviously, Jeff delighted in the "have fun" part of his "Work Hard, Have Fun, Make History" slogan. He made sure his company's employees had fun, too. For example, those who worked in Seattle were once invited to come in costumes to a colorful masquerade ball. There they found Jeff and MacKenzie dressed as butler and maid, with the butler cavorting on the dance floor with a fancy tray that had champagne glasses securely stuck to it.

Such antics seemed to be part of Jeff's good-natured makeup. He could, and often did, bring audiences to roaring applause as he read one of his favorite children's books, *The Stinky Cheese Man,* for the Read Across America program. No company cookout (held for employees every Friday afternoon in summertime) was complete without his taking his turn at grilling hamburgers or playing

kickball. He always had a camera handy and shot dozens of photos, often several rolls a day. "I do it," he said, "because keeping a written diary takes too much energy. This way, 50 years from now, I may have some hope of reconstructing my life. In my closet, I have boxes and boxes of pictures."

Relaxed, Funny, and Humble

America's business magazines keep a close watch on young executives and fast-growing businesses. By 2001 three leading publications had summed up their opinions of Jeff Bezos and, at the same time, captured his personality. "With a genial manner," said *BusinessWeek*, "he seems an unlikely E-commerce mogul. Yet he has made almost no visible missteps since he conceived the idea."

Forbes magazine's opinion was: "Bezos handles success well. A genuinely nice guy who's kept his sense of humor in the face of intense pressure. Also one of the smartest guys in the business."

"It's almost impossible to be in the same room with Bezos and not have a good time," said *Fortune*. "He's relaxed, he's funny, and he's disarmingly humble."

Business experts admired three of Amazon.com's innovations in particular. They liked the fact that zShops made it possible for any firm—large or small, local or worldwide—to sell its merchandise on Amazon.com. Second, they respected the convenience of Amazon.com's patented 1-Click payment feature. And third, they prized the website's All Products Search, a cyber "engine" that enabled a customer to find anything for sale anywhere on the Internet. "This is a win for customers," said Jeff, "who get bigger selections, a win for sellers, who can now reach more customers hassle-free, and a win for Amazon.com because we're now an even better shopping destination. This is all about finding what you want and saving time and money."

The growth continued. During 2001, Amazon.com's database included 30 million customers worldwide and offered 18 million different items for sale in its many categories from software to kitchen products, from DVDs to books, from patio and lawn items to video games and electronics.

In the summer of 2002, editors from *BusinessWeek* reminded Jeff that Steve Case, the founder of America Online, had said that the day would come when e-mail would simply be called mail. Would e-commerce, they asked, just become known as commerce? "It's certainly the goal of any new technology," said Jeff, "to become an old technology. When you fly across the country or across the Atlantic Ocean, nobody thinks anymore, 'This is amazing, that I can be in London in six hours.' Or that you can pick up a phone and call anyone anywhere in the world. We take it for granted. Of course, that's what you want for e-commerce to ultimately become—a part of everyday life, that people think of it as if they were going to the grocery store."

Jeff offered another thought on that point. As computers get cheaper and cheaper, he said, "people will start to have multiple computers in their homes. If you were to install a computer in your kitchen, your Amazon

Jeff shakes hands with another pioneer, Microsoft chairman Bill Gates, inventor of the Windows operating system, at a charity tennis game. Tennis stars Andre Agassi (back right) and Pete Sampras also played in the doubles match.
(Associated Press)

purchases would probably double. That's what happened in my house."

In the fall of 2002 and spring of 2003, still more categories were added. Now customers could shop directly for clothes from Land's End, Gap, Nordstrom, and hundreds of other retailers. And they could buy any of 3,000 brand names in sporting goods. Altogether, Amazon.com was filling $1 billion worth of orders every three months.

Patent and Profit

On February 25, 2003, United States Patent 6,525,747 was issued to Jeffrey P. Bezos of Seattle. It gave him and Amazon.com Inc. (the company to which he assigned the patent) full ownership of the "method and system for conducting a discussion relating to an item" described in his patent application back on August 2, 1999. Getting the patent meant that no other company could use Amazon.com's system for handling sales on the Internet. In a sense, such recognition by the established government authority also meant that Amazon.com had graduated from youth into adulthood.

In October 2003 Jeff announced that Amazon.com had closed the third quarter of the year with a net profit. His company was, at last, earning more than it spent. Its stock, which had been selling for about $20 per share in

January, was now back at a high level, selling for more than $61 in October.

During the year, Jeff sold some of his own millions of shares in his company. Those he sold in November alone gave him more than $50 million before the stock price dropped back to $48 per share in December. And he still owned more than 105 million shares.

On September 15, 2003, *Fortune*, the magazine that regularly keeps track of the size of companies and the wealth of business people, announced the "40 Under 40: Richest"—the 40 Americans less than 40 years old who had the most money. Now 39 years old, Jeff Bezos was ranked third. (The year before, he had been fourth.) The magazine said his net worth—that is, the money he would have if all his personal debts were paid—was $4.85 billion. A year earlier, it had been $1.66 billion. Having oodles of money, however, did not change Jeff's personality or outlook. Back when he was first listed by *Forbes* magazine as one of the 400 richest Americans, he had good-naturedly said that the only real difference in his life was that he no longer had to look at the prices on a menu.

October 23 brought an announcement from Amazon .com that startled the world of authors and publishers. For months, said the company, it had been creating a digital archive of more than 120,000 books, totaling 33 million pages. That meant it had scanned every page of all those books, turning them into cyber data. Whoever went to Amazon.com and clicked on a book marked "Search Inside" or "Look Inside" could see specific pages.

Publishers and authors were furious. They accused Amazon.com of violating the copyrights they held on the books. But Jeff Bezos pointed out that a search of a digitized book simply showed pictures of pages. The viewer could browse backward or forward for a few pages but could not download or copy them. Nor could anyone read the book from first page to last. The idea of "Search Inside the Book" was not to give away the book but rather to provide information about it. "It is critical," said Jeff, "that this be understood as a way to get publishers and authors in contact with customers. We're perfectly aligned with these folks. Our goal is to sell more books."

A Profitable Year

For Jeff Bezos and his company, the 2003 holiday season produced numbers he and MacKenzie had hardly dared dream at Christmas nine years earlier. On its busiest day, Amazon.com had seen 2.1 million items ordered. That is 24 per second or 1,440 every minute, worldwide. More than 1 million packages had been shipped on the busiest warehouse day. On December 24 alone, more than 70,000 gift certificates had been ordered for e-mail delivery in time for Christmas. And during a single hour on December 15, an all-time record had been set by 630,000 visitors clicking on Amazon.com.

In January 2004, at the start of the national election year, Amazon.com added to its long history of making unexpected announcements. Anyone who wanted to contribute to political campaigns, it said, could do so on Amazon.com with a credit card and the click of a mouse. "We're making it as easy for people to contribute," said the website, "as it is to buy the latest 'Harry Potter.'" The site listed presidential candidates in alphabetical order, including a statement on policy and a brief biography for each. While the law allows an individual to give a candidate as much as $2,000, Amazon.com asked for contributions to be kept from $5 to $200.

Next came the announcement that all Wall Street and countless other business people had been waiting and hoping for. For the first time since its inception, said a *New York Times* story on January 28, 2004, Amazon.com earned a full-year profit in 2003: $35 million. Sales in the company's fourth quarter, in fact, were 36 percent more than a year earlier, totaling $1.95 billion. In effect, said the story, Amazon.com "has secured a position as one of the best known brand names on the Internet."

When that good news came out, Jeff Bezos had just celebrated his 40th birthday.

It Does Not Change Human Nature

If you go to see Jeff Bezos at his door desk in his office, you will find he does not look like the typical businessman. His everyday dress code is khaki pants, a deep blue shirt, and no jacket, unless he is making a more formal appearance somewhere, in which case he dons a navy blue or black blazer—but no necktie. "I wear the same thing every weekday," he said in an interview in January 2002, "and I have for ten years. I don't like to think about what I want to wear in the morning. You should definitely stay away from asking me fashion questions."

Jeff likes to walk out of his office and stroll through Seattle's downtown business section. Much as he prizes the way Amazon.com serves its online customers, he also enjoys shopping in retail stores. "I'm an extrovert," he says. "I like seeing other people. I like seeing what they're buying. I like touching things. I like smelling things. The physical world is still the best medium ever invented. It's a great way to do things. The Internet changes a lot of stuff. But one very important thing it does not change is human nature."

He hurries along the street, darting through a late-afternoon throng of shoppers. "You see," he says, "none of this is going away. The Net can't replace this experience."

Jeff continues to encourage the people who work in his company to "Work Hard, Have Fun, Make History." And

Jeff says he is proud that Amazon.com has, "raised the bar on customer experience for every industry all over the world." (Associated Press)

by following that credo, he and his company have made history. As Jeff sees it, "What I would really like people to say about Amazon is that we raised the bar on customer experience for every industry all over the world."

The people who work hard and have fun at Amazon.com continue to admire their leader. "There was always a certain comfort in hearing him laugh," says one, "especially during the heavy growth phase, which was difficult. It was nice knowing that he was there and that he was as involved as you were. That's part of his being the soul of the company. His laugh is as much the soul as he himself is."

TIME LINE

1964 Born January 12 in Albuquerque, New Mexico, to Jackie Gise

1968 Jackie Gise marries Mike Bezos, who legally adopts Jeff

1976 Builds an Infinity Cube

1980 Wins a trip to the Marshall Space Flight Center

1982 Delivers the valedictory speech at his high school graduation

1984 Works as a programmer/analyst during a summer job in Norway

1985 Improves an IBM program during a summer job in California

1986 Graduates summa cum laude from Princeton University with B.S. in electrical engineering and computer science; becomes member of Phi Beta Kappa; joins the FITEL high-technology company in New York City

1988   Joins Bankers Trust Company

1990   Joins D.E. Shaw & Co.

1992   Becomes Shaw's youngest senior vice president

1993   Marries MacKenzie Tuttle

1994   Moves to Seattle and creates Amazon.com

1995   Launches Amazon.com on the Internet, selling books

1996   *Wall Street Journal* runs a story about Amazon.com

1997   Barnes & Noble sues Amazon.com; Amazon.com's initial public offering (IPO) is $18 per share; 1-Click ordering begins; year's sales total $147 million

1998   Music CDs, videos, and DVDs are sold on Amazon.com; bookselling in the United Kingdom and Germany begins; Shop the Web is announced as "the place to buy anything you want to buy online"; fourth quarter revenue totals $250 million

1999   Five enormous Amazon.com warehouses are built; products and services added include auctions, e-cards, toys and electronics, tools and hardware; 10 millionth customer is served; zShops are introduced; Amazon.com wins an injunction against Barnes & Noble's use of 1-Click technology; Jeff Bezos is named *Time*'s Person of the Year

2000 First Amazon.com job layoffs occur; products added include patio furniture, health and beauty aids, and kitchenware; Amazon.co.jp opens in Japan and Amazon.fr starts in France; end of year sales are $2.76 billion, with 20 million customers served; Jeff and MacKenzie's son, Preston, is born

2001 In uniform, Jeff delivers the first CD-video order to a Japanese family; by end of year 30 million customers served worldwide

2002 Clothing sales are added

2003 Sporting-goods are added; Amazon.com announces its first-ever third-quarter net profit

2004 Amazon.com announces a program to handle contributions to presidential candidates' campaigns; announcement that 2003 showed Amazon.com's first full-year profit

HOW TO BECOME AN INTERNET ENTREPRENEUR

THE JOB

In spite of the failure of many high-profile dot-coms in the early 2000s, many online businesses have continued to survive and thrive. These "e-tailers" have adapted to the constantly changing technology, economic climate, business trends, and consumer demands, instead of concentrating on fast growth and offering the lowest prices. Reports by research firm Jupiter Communications show that consumers are using Internet stores to do comparison shopping; a significant number of consumers research products online before buying them at traditional stores. Jupiter Communications predicts that the amount spent by consumers for online purchases and Web-influenced purchases at traditional stores will soon top $831 billion.

Because of the vastness of the Internet, the role of an *Internet entrepreneur* or an *Internet store manager* can vary as much as the numerous websites on the Internet. Expert opinion on what makes one website or one business more successful than another differs, too. E-commerce is a new and relatively unexplored field for entrepreneurs. But because most entrepreneurs have innovative and creative natures, this uncertainty and uncharted territory is what they love.

Like traditional entrepreneurs, Internet entrepreneurs must have strong business skills. They come up with ideas for an Internet product or service, research the feasibility of selling this product or service, decide what they need to charge to make a profit, determine how to advertise their business, and even arrange for financing for their business if necessary. In addition, Internet entrepreneurs are typically computer savvy and may even create and maintain their own sites.

Some entrepreneurs may choose to market a service, such as website design, to target the business-to-business market. Other Internet entrepreneurs may decide to market a service, such as computer dating, to target the individual consumer market. Still others may develop a

"virtual store" on the Internet and sell products that target businesses or individual consumers.

Internet stores vary in size, items for sale, and the range of products. Smaller Internet stores, for example, may market the work done by a single craftsperson or businessperson. Many large Internet stores focus on selling a specific product or line of products. As some of these stores have grown they have diversified their merchandise. Amazon.com is one such example. Originally a small, online bookstore, the company now sells music, videos, household items, electronics, and clothing in addition to books. Other Internet stores, such as those of Eddie Bauer and Sears, may be extensions of catalog or traditional brick-and-mortar stores. These large companies are generally so well established that they can employ Internet store managers to oversee the virtual store.

Many Internet businesses begin small, with one person working as the owner, manager, webmaster, marketing director, and accountant, among other positions. John Axne of Chicago, Illinois, took on all these responsibilities when he developed his own one-person business designing websites for small companies and corporations. "Having my own business allows me more creative freedom," says Axne. The successful Internet entrepreneur, like the successful traditional entrepreneur, is often able to combine his or her interests with work to fill a niche in the business world. "It's a great fit for me," Axne explains. "I have a passion for computers and a love of learning. This business allows me to sell myself and my services." Dave Wright of Venice, California, is also an Internet entrepreneur and website designer. He, too, combined his interests with computer skills to start his business. "I had a strong interest in art," he says. "I simply married my art and graphic art experience with computers."

Those who want to start their own businesses on the Web must be very focused and self-motivated. Just like any other entrepreneur, they always need to keep an eye on the competition to see what products and services as well as prices and delivery times others offer. While Internet entrepreneurs do not need to be computer whizzes, they should enjoy learning about technology so that they can keep up with new developments that may help them with their businesses. Internet entrepreneurs must also be decision makers, and many are drawn to running their own businesses because of the control it offers. "I'm a control freak," Wright admits. "This way I can oversee every aspect of my job."

The typical day of the Internet store manager or entrepreneur will depend greatly on the company he or she works for. Someone who works for a large company that also has a Web store, for example, may meet with company department heads to find out about upcoming sales or products that should be heavily advertised on the website. They may do research about the store use and report their findings to company managers. They may work on the site itself, updating it with new information.

The Internet entrepreneur also has varied responsibilities that depend on his or her business. Wright notes, "No two projects and no two days are alike." An entrepreneur may spend one day working with a client to determine the client's needs and the next day working on bookkeeping and advertising in addition to working on a project. Most entrepreneurs, however, enjoy this variety and flexibility.

While the Internet world is appealing to many, there are risks for those who start their own businesses. "The Internet changes so rapidly that in five years it may be entirely different," Wright says. "That's why I started a business that simply sells services and didn't require a major investment. It is a business that I can get into and out of quickly if I find it necessary. There is no product, per se, and no inventory." Despite uncertainties, however, Web stores continue to open and the number of Internet store managers and entrepreneurs continues to grow.

REQUIREMENTS

High School

If you are considering becoming an Internet entrepreneur or Internet store manager, there are a number of classes you can take in high school to help prepare you for these careers. Naturally you should take computer science courses to give you a familiarity with using computers and the Web. Business and marketing courses will also help you. Also, take mathematics, accounting, or bookkeeping classes because, as an entrepreneur, you will be responsible for your company's finances. Take history classes to learn about economic trends and psychology classes to learn about human behavior. A lot of advertising and product promotion has a psychological element. Finally, take plenty of English classes. These classes will help you develop your communication skills, which will be vital to your work as a store manager or business owner.

Postsecondary Training

Although there are no specific educational requirements for Internet entrepreneurs, a college education will certainly enhance your skills and chances for success. Like anyone interested in working for or running a traditional business, take plenty of business, economics, and marketing and management classes. Your education should also include accounting or bookkeeping classes. Keep up with computer and Internet developments by taking computer classes. Some schools offer classes on e-commerce. Many schools have undergraduate degree programs in business or business administration, but you can also enter this field with other degrees. Dave Wright, for example, graduated with a degree from art school, while John Axne has degrees in biomedical engineering and interactive media.

Certification or Licensing

Licenses may be required for running a business, depending on the type of business. Since requirements vary, you will need to check with local and state agencies for regulations in your area.

Other Requirements

Internet entrepreneurs and Internet store managers must have the desire and initiative to keep up on new technology and business trends. Because they must deal with many different people in various lines of work, they need to be flexible problem-solvers and have strong communication skills. Creativity and insight into new and different ways of doing business are qualities that are essential for an entrepreneur to be successful. In addition, because the Internet and e-commerce are relatively new and the future of Internet businesses is uncertain, those who enter the field are generally risk-takers and eager to be on the cutting edge of commerce and technology. Dave Wright notes, "This is not a job for someone looking for security. The Internet world is always changing. This is both exciting and scary to me as a businessperson. This is one career where you are not able to see where you will be in five years."

EXPLORING

There are numerous ways in which you can explore your interest in the computer and business worlds. Increase your computer skills and find out how much this technology interests you by joining a computer users group or club at your high school or in your community. Access the Internet frequently to observe different website designs and find out what is being sold and marketed electronically. What sites do you think are best at promoting products and why? Think about things from a customer's point of view. How easy are the sites to access and use? How are the products displayed and accessed? How competitive are the prices for goods or services?

Make it a goal to come up with your own ideas for a product or service to market on the Web, and then do some research. How difficult would it be to deliver the product? What type of financing would be involved? Are there other sites already providing this product or service? How could you make your business unique?

Talk to professionals in your community about their work. Set up informational interviews with local business owners to find out what is involved in starting and running a traditional business. Your local Chamber of Commerce or the Small Business Administration may have classes or publications that would help you learn about starting a business. In addition, set up informational interviews with computer consultants, website designers, or Internet store managers or owners. How did they get started? What advice do they have? Is there anything they wish they had done differently? Where do they see the future of e-commerce going?

If your school has a future business owners club, join this group to meet others with similar interests. For hands-on business experience, get a part-time or summer job at any type of store in your area. This work will give you the opportunity to deal with customers (who can sometimes be hard to please), work with handling money, and observe how the store promotes its products and services.

EMPLOYERS

Entrepreneurs are self-employed, and sometimes they may employ people to work under them. Some Internet entrepreneurs may be hired to begin a business for someone else. Internet store managers may work for an established traditional business or institution that also has a website dealing with products and services. The manager may also work for a business that only has a presence on the Web or for an Internet entrepreneur.

STARTING OUT

Professionals in the field advise those just starting out to work for someone else to gain experience in the business world before beginning their own business. The Internet is a good employment resource. There are many sites that post job openings. Local employment agencies and news-papers and trade magazines also list job opportunities. In addition, your college placement office should be able to provide you with help locating a job. Networking with col-lege alumni and people in your computer users groups may also provide job leads.

ADVANCEMENT

Advancement opportunities depend on the business, its success, and the individual's goals. Internet entrepreneurs or store managers who are successful may enter other business fields or consulting, or they may advance to higher level management positions or other larger Internet-based businesses. Some entrepreneurs establish a business and then sell it only to begin another business venture. The Internet world is constantly changing because of technological advancements. This state of flux means that a wide variety of possibilities are available to those working in the field. "There is no solid career path in the Internet field," says Dave Wright. "Your next career may not even be developed yet."

EARNINGS

Income for Internet store managers and entrepreneurs is usually tied to the profitability of the business. Internet store managers who work for established traditional businesses are typically salaried employees of the company. Internet entrepreneurs who offer a service may be paid by the project. Entrepreneurs are self-employed and their income will depend on the success of the business. Those just starting out may actually have no earnings, while those with a business that has been in existence for several years may have annual earnings between $25,000 and $50,000. Some in the field may earn much more than this amount. John Axne estimates that those who have good technical skills and can do such things as create the database program for a website may have higher salaries, in the $60,000–$125,000 range.

Entrepreneurs are almost always responsible for their own medical, disability, and life insurances. Retirement plans must also be self-funded and self-directed. Internet store managers may or may not receive benefits.

WORK ENVIRONMENT

Internet entrepreneurs and store managers may work out of a home or private office. Some Internet store managers may be required to work on-site at a corporation or small business.

The entrepreneur must deal with the stresses of starting a business, keeping it going, dealing with deadlines and customers, and coping with problems as they arise. They must also work long hours to develop and manage their business venture; many entrepreneurs work over 40 hours a week. Evening or weekend work may also be required, both for the entrepreneur and the store manager.

In addition, these professionals must spend time researching, reading, and checking out the competition in order to be informed about the latest technology and business trends. Their intensive computer work can result in eyestrain, hand and wrist injuries, and back pain.

OUTLOOK

Online commerce is a very new and exciting field with tremendous potential, and it is likely that growth will continue over the long term. However, it is important to keep in mind that the failure rate for new businesses, even traditional ones, is fairly high. A large percentage of dot-coms continue to close or be acquired by other companies. The survivors are small businesses that are able to find niche markets, anticipate trends, adapt to market and technology changes, and plan for a large enough financial margin to turn a profit. Analysts also anticipate that the amount of business-to-business e-commerce will surpass business-to-consumer sales.

Internet managers and entrepreneurs with the most thorough education and experience and who have done their research will have the best opportunities for success. For those who are adventurous and interested in using new avenues for selling products and services, the Internet offers many possibilities.

TO LEARN MORE ABOUT INTERNET ENTREPRENEURS

BOOKS

Carroll, Jim, and Rick Broadhead. *Selling Online*. Chicago: Dearborn, 2001.

Cohen, Adam. *The Perfect Store: Inside eBay*. New York: Little Brown & Company, 2002.

Green, Jim. *Starting an Internet Business at Home*. London: Kogan Page Ltd., 2001.

Mariotti, Steven. *The Young Entrepreneur's Guide to Starting and Running a Business*. New York: Three Rivers Press, 2000.

Strauss, Steven D. *Business Start-up Kit*. Chicago: Dearborn, 2002.

ORGANIZATIONS AND WEBSITES

For information about the information technology industry and e-commerce, contact

Information Technology Association of America

1401 Wilson Boulevard, Suite 1100

Arlington, VA 22209

Tel: 703-522-5055

http://www.itaa.org

The Small Business Administration offers helpful information on starting a business. For information on state offices and additional references, check out their website.

Small Business Administration

409 Third Street, SW

Washington, DC 20416

Tel: 800-827-5722

Email: answerdesk@sba.gov

http://www.sba.gov

Check out the following online magazine specializing in topics of interest to entrepreneurs.

Entrepreneur.com

http://www.entrepreneurmag.com

For resources on information technology careers and computer programming, check out the following website:

Mainfunction.com

http://www.mainfunction.com

TO LEARN MORE ABOUT JEFF BEZOS

BOOKS AND ARTICLES

Buechner, Maryanne Murray. "Waiting for Wal-Mart." *Time*, December 27, 1999.

Brackett, Virginia. *Jeff Bezos*. Philadelphia: Chelsea House Publishers, 2001.

Carlson, Margaret. "A Dinner @ Margaret's." *Time*, December 27, 1999.

Garty, Judy. *Jeff Bezos: Business Genius of Amazon*. Berkeley Heights, New Jersey: Enslow Publishers, Inc., 2003.

Greenfeld, Karl Taro. "Clicks and Bricks." *Time*, December 27, 1999.

Krantz, Michael. "Cruising Inside Amazon." *Time*, December 27, 1999.

Quittner, Joshua. "On the Future." *Time*, December 27, 1999.

Ramo, Joshua Cooper. "It's one of those perfect autumn nights . . ." *Time*, December 27, 1999.

Saunders, Rebecca. *Business the Amazon.com Way: Secrets of the World's Most Astonishing Web Business*. Oxford, England, United Kingdom: Capstone Publishing Limited (A Wiley Company), 2001.

Sherman, Joseph. *Jeff Bezos: King of Amazon*. Brookfield, Connecticut: The Millbrook Press, 2001.

Spector, Robert. *Amazon.com Get Big Fast*. New York: HarperBusiness, 2002.

Taylor, Chris. "Web-Free Shopping." *Time*, December 27, 1999.

———. "Food Fight! Food Fight!" *Time*, December 27, 1999.

Zeff, Joe. "From Your Mouse to Your House." *Time*, December 27, 1999.

INTERNET SOURCES

"40 Under 40: Richest." *Fortune*, September 15, 2003.

"The Fantasy World of Jeff Bezos." *Red Herring*, October 1, 2000. Available online. URL: http://www.redherring

.com/Article.aspx?f=Articles/Archive/mag/issue83/ mag-bezos-83.xml&hed = The%20fantasy%20 world%20of%20Jeff%20Bezos. Downloaded February 1, 2004.

"Jeff Bezos." *Wikipedia, the free encyclopedia,* January 9, 2004. Available online. URL: http://en.wikipedia.org/ w/wiki.phtml?title = Jeff_Bezos&printable = yes. Downloaded February 1, 2004.

"Method and system for conducting a discussion relating to an item." United States Patent 6,525,747, Bezos, February 25, 2003. Available online. URL: http:/patft. uspto.gov/netacgi/nph-Parser?Sect1 = PTO1&Sect2 = HITOFF&d = PALL&p = 1&u = /netahtml/srchnum.htm &r = 1&f = G&1 = 50&s1 = 6,525,747.WKU.&OS = PN/6,52 5,747&RS = PN/6,525,747. Downloaded February 1, 2004.

"Newsmakers of 2003: Jeff Bezos." *Puget Sound Business Journal,* December 26, 2003. Available online. URL: http://www.bizjournals.com/seattle/stories/2003/12/ 29/focus3.html?t = printable. Downloaded February 1, 2004.

"Plugged In: Jeff Bezos the space oddity." *St. Paul Pioneer Press,* May 5, 2003. Available online. URL: http://www .twincities.com/mld/pioneerpress/business/technology/ 5779275.htm. Posted May 5, 2003.

Bayers, Chip. "The Inner Bezos." *Wired,* March 1999. Available online. URL: http://www.wired.com/wired/ archive/7.03/bezos_pr.html. Downloaded February 1, 2004.

Dembeck, Chet. "A Kinder, Gentler Jeff Bezos?" *E-Commerce Times,* March 13, 2000. Available online. URL: http:// www.ecommercetimes.com/perl/story/2719.html. Downloaded February 1, 2004.

Fishman, Charles. "Face Time With Jeff Bezos." *Fast-Company,* February 2001. Available online. URL: http:// www.fastcompany.com/magazine/43/bezos.html. Downloaded January 26, 2004.

Fussman, Cal. "Jeff Bezos, Founder and CEO of Amazon.com, 37, Seattle." *Esquire,* January 2002. Available online. URL: http://www.esquire.com/cgi-bin/ printtool/print. cgi?pages = 1&filename = %2Ffeatures%2Flear... Downloaded March 29, 2004.

Hansell, Saul. "The Search for the Perfect Gift: Just a Click, Not a Drive, Away." *The New York Times*, December 3, 2003.

———. "Amazon Reports First Full-Year Profit." *The New York Times*, January 28, 2004.

Hardy, Pat Esclavon. "Jeff Bezos and Amazon.com: Can Earth's Biggest Bookstore Make It?" *StarIQ*, 2001. Available online. URL: http://www.stariq.com/pagetemplate/article-printer.asp?pageid=1966. Downloaded February 2, 2004.

Hof, Robert D. "Jeffrey P. Bezos." *BusinessWeek.com*, September 27, 1999. Available online. URL: http://www.businessweek.com/1999/99_39/b3648004.htm. Downloaded February 1, 2004.

Justice, Glen. "Chance to Give Via Amazon." *The New York Times*, January 25, 2004.

Levinson, Meridith. "Jeff Bezos." *CIO Magazine*, October 1, 2002. Available online. URL: http://www.cio.com/archive/100102/honoree_inv_bezos.html?printversion=yes. Downloaded February 1, 2004.

Mason, Paul. "Jeff Bezos." *BBC News,* October 8, 2002. Available online. URL: http://news.bbc.co.uk/2/hi/ programmes/newsnight/archive/2310543.stm. Downloaded March 29, 2004.

O'Connell, Patricia, ed. "Chewing the Sashimi with Jeff Bezos." *BusinessWeek online,* July 15, 2002. Available online. URL: http://www.businessweek.com:/print/ bwdaily/dnflash/jul2002/nf20020715_5066.htm?db. Downloaded March 29, 2004.

O'Reilly, Tim. "My Conversation with Jeff Bezos." *The O'Reilly Network,* March 2, 2000. Available online. URL: http://www.oreilly.com/lpt/a/3630. Downloaded February 1, 2004.

Shook, David. "Jeff Bezos: Finally Relaxing?" *BusinessWeek. com,* October 1, 2002. Available online. URL: http:// www.businessweek.com/technology/content/oct2002/ tc2002101_9694.htm. Downloaded February 1, 2004.

Sippy, Michael. "Questions for Jeff Bezos." *Stating the Obvious,* October 14, 1996. Available online. URL: http:// www.theobvious.com/archive/1996/10/14.html. Downloaded February 1, 2004.

Wolf, Gary. "The Great Library of Amazonia." *Wired,* December 2003. Available online. URL: http://www .wired.com/news/print/0,1294,60948,00.html. Downloaded March 29, 2004.

INDEX

Page numbers in *italics* indicate illustrations.